# JACKSONIAN DEMOCRACY
# ON THE FLORIDA FRONTIER

*by Arthur W. Thompson*

University of Florida Monographs
SOCIAL SCIENCES
No. 9, Winter 1961

# JACKSONIAN DEMOCRACY
# ON THE FLORIDA FRONTIER

*by Arthur W. Thompson*

University of Florida Monographs
## SOCIAL SCIENCES
## No. 9, Winter 1961

UNIVERSITY OF FLORIDA PRESS / GAINESVILLE, FLORIDA

COPYRIGHT, 1961, BY THE BOARD OF
COMMISSIONERS OF STATE INSTITUTIONS
OF FLORIDA

LIBRARY OF CONGRESS
CATALOGUE CARD NO. 61-63107

PRINTED BY THE BULKLEY-NEWMAN PRINTING COMPANY
TALLAHASSEE, FLORIDA

# PREFACE

Jacksonian historiography has tended to place its primary emphasis, during the past century, on the national scene. Only in recent years have historians devoted more of their attention to some of the more detailed developments on the local level. This study is intended, therefore, not only as a contribution to Florida history, but also as a modest piece toward filling in one of the many gaps in the Jacksonian mosaic.

Because of rigid space limitations, the basic focus is on the Florida frontier itself, with interactive trends and relationships between national and state activities kept to an absolute minimum. Again, space limitations have dictated that the footnotes must also serve as a somewhat fragmented bibliography. All manuscripts, unless otherwise noted, as well as all newspapers referred to, are in the Library of Florida History at the University of Florida.

The author wishes to express his deepest thanks to Mr. Julien C. Yonge, Director Emeritus of the P. K. Yonge Library of Florida History, for bringing that prime collection of Floridiana together, as well as for placing it so completely and generously at his disposal. Acknowledgements must also go to Rembert W. Patrick for his careful reading of the manuscript and the constructive suggestions which followed, and to my wife, Irene S. Thompson, for accepting a host of burdens beyond the original marriage contract.

ARTHUR W. THOMPSON

GAINESVILLE, FLORIDA
FEBRUARY, 1961

# CONTENTS

# 1. BACKGROUND
# AND ORIGINS

In March, 1840, a St. Augustine Democratic newspaper proclaimed, "In Florida as everywhere else, two parties exist."[1] It is possible, of course, that all the implications of the statement were not perceived at that moment. Still, no one then in the nation's southernmost territory would have challenged its validity, least of all the startled and apprehensive leaders among the opposition conservatives. It was more than a statement of faith; it was the elucidation of a fact. It announced, in effect, that the American political process had finally come to the Florida frontier. Where for nearly two decades there had been only political "ins," there were now both "ins" and "outs," with the latter increasingly assuming the status of the former.

For some in Florida the emergence of a full-blown, effectively functioning two-party system was a tragedy. Dire warnings of the insidious influence of factions which had been intoned by some of the "founding fathers" were hastily resurrected, but to no avail. The real tragedy, however, was not the appearance of this political mechanism, but its virtual disappearance within another two decades.

It is the intention of this paper to demonstrate that in Florida "in the beginning"—1821—there was Jackson, but no Jacksonian Democrats; "in the hour of triumph"—1841—there were Jacksonian Democrats, but no Jackson; and "in the end"—1861—there were neither Jacksonian Democrats nor Jackson.

## THE "JACKSON MEN"

On March 12, 1821, Secretary of State John Quincy Adams sent Andrew Jackson his commission as military governor of Florida. For Jackson's followers it was a moment of rejoicing. Not only had the General's earlier precipitate action been vindicated, but the appointment would provide him with a glorious opportunity to pay old debts. President Monroe, however, had his own quota of political debts, and some of the Florida patronage was dispensed without consultation with the new governor. This infuriated Jackson because,

1. *Florida Herald*, March 5, 1840.

1

as his secretary, Andrew J. Donelson, wrote, "one motive for accepting the governorship was the promotion and assistance of his friends."[2]

Still, the territory was new, the slate relatively clean, and a host of positions remained. Jackson made a substantial contribution toward filling this political vacuum. Many of his cronies, enjoying the fruits of expansionism, were appointed to a variety of posts, including those of territorial secretary, surveyor general, register of the land office, and agents to conduct land sales. Many became district judges, district attorneys, and postmasters; others found memberships on the strategic board of land commissioners; a goodly number moved in as clerks in sundry territorial offices; and still others contented themselves with local positions.[3] Of the Jackson men who migrated to the new southern frontier during these early days, none would become more influential than Richard Keith Call. Moreover, Jackson's brief tenure as a senator from Tennessee between 1823 and 1825, happily coinciding with Call's single term as territorial delegate from Florida, provided further opportunity to bolster the Jackson contingent on the local scene.[4]

From the few early intramural quarrels among Jackson's Florida satellites, Richard Call quickly emerged as West Florida's key leader.[5] The only real political irritant for the Jackson clan at that time was Joseph M. White who, as a member of the board of land commissioners, uncovered some land frauds in the territory. His ardent defense of the "yeoman farmer," coupled with the fact that he was a skilled politician who supported the land claims of the Spanish

2. John W. Ward, *Andrew Jackson: Symbol for an Age* (New York, 1955), p. 63; Herbert J. Doherty, Jr., "The Governorship of Andrew Jackson," *Florida Historical Quarterly*, XXXIII (July, 1954), 9.

3. Rembert W. Patrick, *Florida Under Five Flags* (Gainesville, Fla., 1955), p. 31; Doherty, "Andrew Jackson's Cronies in Florida Territorial Politics," *Florida Historical Quarterly*, XXXIV (July, 1955), 4-6; Tallahassee *Florida Advocate*, February 14, 1829; James O. Knauss, *Territorial Florida Journalism* (DeLand, Fla., 1926), pp. 23-24, 63-64; Pensacola *Gazette*, April 9, 1825; John S. Bassett, *Correspondence of Andrew Jackson* (7 vols.; Washington, 1926-35), III, 229; Rowland H. Rerick, *Memoirs of Florida* (2 vols.; Atlanta, 1902), I, 175, 188; *Dictionary of American Biography* (22 vols.; New York, 1928-58), VII, 83-84; A. Jackson to J. Bronaugh, August 27, 1822 (Miscellaneous Jackson Papers, P. K. Yonge Library of Florida History, University of Florida).

4. St. Augustine *East Florida Herald*, September 27, 1823; Tallahassee *Florida Advocate*, February 14, 1829; Knauss, *Journalism*, pp. 23-24, 63-64; Pensacola *Gazette*, April 9, 1825; Bassett, *Jackson Correspondence*, III, 229.

5. West Florida at this time included the area west of the Suwannee River.

inhabitants and fought for internal improvements, made possible not only his victory in 1825 over James Gadsden, the Jackson group's candidate for delegate to Congress, but also his re-election on five successive occasions until his voluntary retirement in 1837.[6]

Despite the disconcerting shadow cast by Delegate White, political and economic affairs within the territory remained firmly in the hands of the Jackson appointees and followers. Like-minded individuals, many of them from Virginia, continued to flow into the area during the twenties and the early thirties, building up the strength of the original band. "The Nucleus," as this group was commonly referred to, entrenched itself across the northern settled tier of the territory from St. Augustine to Pensacola. Power, however, tended to be focused in the geographic center of this area, in Tallahassee and populous Leon County. Here the speculators and the "land-office crowd" held sway. Supporting Richard Call's leadership were large land speculators such as Richard C. Allen; prominent planters such as William B. Nuttall; legal talent such as George K. Walker and George T. Ward; land-office officials such as Robert Butler, Isham G. Searcy, and Robert W. Williams; newspaper editors such as Ambrose Crane, Algernon S. Thruston, Edgar Macon, and Leslie A. Thompson.[7]

In the course of time many of these men and similarly oriented figures acquired from their land speculation not only some ready capital, but also sizeable holdings. The next step, the transition to a more stable and respectable occupation, led them almost inevitably into the slaveholding, cotton-plantation group during the latter part of the 1820's and much of the following decade.

The gradual emergence of this group of large plantations directed its members' attention to new interests. Internal improvements on a large scale would be needed; more important perhaps, and certainly more immediate, was the urge to expand their slave holdings. In either case, the banking institution appeared to be a logical candidate for addition to the territorial scene. Relatively little was done in the way of internal improvement during the territorial era. The establishment of banks in each of the three centers of the territory,

6. Pensacola *Gazette*, January 6, 1827; Doherty, *The Whigs of Florida, 1845-1854* (Gainesville, Fla., 1959), p. 2; Sidney W. Martin, *Florida During Territorial Days* (Athens, Ga., 1944), p. 48; Doherty, "Jackson's Cronies," p. 15.

7. "Jackson's Cronies," pp. 15-16; Knauss, *Journalism*, pp. 23-24, 65-66, 103-04.

3

however, contributed enormously to the economic position of these early leaders. Ironically, the policies and consequences of these same banks, in turn, contributed to their political collapse.

Early agitation led to the establishment of the Bank of Pensacola in 1831. But it was Governor William P. DuVal whose message in 1833 to the Legislative Council broke new ground. He called for the establishment of a "planter bank," and added, "to meet my approval it must be in fact as well as in name the planters' bank."[8] And so, by and large, it would be after the charter of the Union Bank of Tallahassee was finally approved on February 13 of that same year.[9] The Union Bank, chartered for forty years, was the largest and most influential of the three financial institutions created in the early thirties. Its capitalization was initially set at $1,000,000. Subscriptions were sold to landowners who secured their stock purchases with twenty-year mortgages on land, slaves, and homes. A government-appointed board would in each instance set the value of such security. Obviously this was a fairly happy arrangement for the planters, but it did exceedingly little to provide the bank with any working capital. Hard cash would come from the sale of one thousand $1,000 bonds to be issued by the territory and sold by the bank at par. Within a year the bank could raise its capitalization to $3,000,000 and the government would obligingly provide another two thousand $1,000 bonds. These securities were payable in twenty-four to thirty years and were backed by the faith of the territorial government.[10]

Similar arrangements had been made for the Bank of Pensacola, which received $500,000 in bonds, and for the Southern Life Insurance and Trust Company in St. Augustine which acquired $400,000 worth under its charter of 1835. In no time at all the Nucleus of Florida had apparently committed the territory to over $2,000,000 worth of what were called "faith bonds."[11]

To facilitate the sale of these bonds, legal opinions were solicited from a number of prominent Americans. Those who obliged with favorable responses were Chancellor Kent, Peter Jay, Horace Binney, and Daniel Webster. All four of these gentlemen agreed that

8. Florida *Legislative Council Journal* (1833), pp. 5-6.
9. For further details on the bank laws see Kathryn Abbey, "The Union Bank of Tallahassee," *Florida Historical Quarterly*, XV (April, 1937), 207-31.
10. *Ibid.*, p. 209; St. Augustine *Florida Herald*, April 24, 1843.
11. The balance of the bonds authorized by the legislature were either not issued or not sold.

the territory possessed the necessary authority to issue such bonds and, moreover, that the bonds constituted a binding contract which could not be invalidated later.[12]

This formidable array of legal talent dispelled any possible doubts and also provided the necessary green light to proceed. Stock sales of the Union Bank were concentrated almost completely in Middle Florida, especially in Leon County. For the sale of the bonds, the followers of Richard Call and the members of the Nucleus who controlled all three banks—particularly the one in Tallahassee—had to go farther afield. Though the banks had been chartered under the leadership of William P. DuVal, most of the bonds were issued by Call himself, whose appointment as governor of the territory in 1836 by President Jackson came at an extremely propitious moment.[13] Apparently with a minimum of dickering, 200 bonds of the Union Bank were sold in New York to J. D. Beers and Company, agents for the American Life and Trust Company.[14] Philadelphia's Nicholas Biddle established contact with Hope and Company in Amsterdam, where another 100 were disposed of. Through Thomas Biddle and Company, 966 were placed in London hands.[15] Baring Brothers evinced some interest, but the firm was cautious and further investigation on its part temporarily halted all European sales. This decision not to acquire any Florida bonds finally surfaced latent suspicions and 704 remained unsold in London. Of all the Union bonds issued, only 30 were purchased by Floridians.[16]

Suspicions had already been aroused a lot closer to home. In Washington national involvement in banking schemes was viewed with something less than cordiality, and the sale of territorial bonds meant possible national involvement. As a consequence, a bill was passed which prohibited the issuance of such bonds withour prior congressional approval.[17]

Something stronger than suspicion had, in the meantime, been

12. Florida *House Journal* (1840), Appendix, pp. 17-26.

13. DuVal served from 1822 to 1834 and was succeeded by John H. Eaton prior to the accession of Call.

14. David Y. Thomas, "A History of Banking in Florida" (unpublished manuscript, Library of Florida History), pp. 33-34.

15. Reginald C. McGrane, "Some Aspects of American State Debts in the Forties," *American Historical Review*, XXXVIII (July, 1933), 674; Henry D. Gilpin, *Statement of the Case of the Bonds and Guarantees Issued by the Territory of Florida* (Philadelphia, 1847), p. 16.

16. Gilpin, p. 16; Apalachicola *Gazette*, October 30, 1839.

17. Abbey, p. 211.

5

aroused in Florida. To begin with, when the Union Bank expanded its stock in order to secure additional cash from the sale of more bonds, 17,000 of the 20,000 new shares went to existing stockholders. The balance was nicely distributed among 152 new subscribers, while 164 would-be owners received nothing.[18] Within a few years the heat generated by party strife threw more light on the operations of the territorial bank.[19]

In addition to the nascent opposition on the economic front, political fissures among the Jackson men themselves began to appear. The break between Andrew Jackson and John C. Calhoun, particularly on the issue of nullification, had local repercussions. The split between Call and James Gadsden reflected this cleavage. Call's Unionism, which he consistently maintained down through the secession crisis of 1861, placed him, for the moment at least, squarely in the Jackson camp.[20] Gadsden's South Carolinian origins, on the other hand, came to the fore. As a consequence, Call replaced the four-time unsuccessful Gadsden as the candidate to attempt to unseat James M. White for congressional delegate in 1833.[21]

This partial estrangement of Jackson's Florida followers in 1833 was made virtually complete with Call's own alienation three years later. Though Call had moved a long way from the "Jacksonian persuasion," he maintained a considerable personal attachment for the man. Meanwhile, the Seminole War, however unpleasant, had provided Call with an opportunity to exercise long-restrained military ambitions. But the bonds of friendship between the two men were strained when Jackson removed General Call from his military command in 1836. Despite Call's earlier appointment as governor, relations between the two men rapidly declined.[22] This personal clash was only part of a deeper cleavage which had developed over the preceding decade. Many of those who remained in Florida had come during Andrew Jackson's brief military governorship, and together with others who followed via his patronage they assumed leadership of the new territory's political and economic affairs. By

18. *Ibid.*, pp. 214-15.   19. *House Journal* (1840), Appendix.

20. For a fine biography of Call see Doherty, "Richard Keith Call: Southern Unionist" (Ph.D. dissertation, University of North Carolina, 1953; to be published by University of Florida Press, fall, 1961).

21. A. Jackson to R. K. Call, July 14, 1833, in "Journal of Governor R. K. Call" (unpublished manuscript, Florida Historical Society), pp. 197-98.

22. Doherty, "Richard Keith Call," p. 231; Clarence E. Carter, *Territorial Papers of the United States*, Vol. XXV, *Florida Territory, 1834-1839* (Washington, 1961), pp. 279, 339-41.

and large, they were able to maintain that control for nearly two decades down through the late 1830's. Yet as Jackson assumed an increasingly new role in the affairs of the nation, his Florida followers were moving in a very different direction. Aside from those who had died or moved to new areas, a large percentage of them progressed into the ranks of the "conservatives." Before long the Nucleus would become the hard core of the Florida Whigs and paradoxically the old "Jackson men" would bitterly oppose the rise of the newer political and economic tendencies embodied in the "Jacksonian Democrats."

## ORIGINS OF THE JACKSONIANS

Prior to 1838, territorial elections operated without the existence of organized political parties. By and large, candidates were selected by legislative caucus or other elite groups and supported on the basis of personality, point of origin, or other individual preference that usually bore little or no relationship to principle or party. Divergent, even conflicting, groups and interests often cooperated on a variety of local issues without reference to factional differences. Still, the party battles of the Jackson era were not unknown to much of the Florida populace.[23] And, despite the preoccupation with the harsh realities of frontier life, neither were the implications of that political struggle. There were some who felt that "the great political war" that had been raging for some years past would "ultimately produce grand results" even in Florida.[24] But somehow that appeared to be in the future and more pressing issues were at hand.

Early in 1837 Governor Call and many of his followers, convinced of the sufficiency of the territory's population and desirous of statehood, pushed for a referendum on that subject. As a consequence, a territorial canvass was conducted in conjunction with the May election for delegate. Middle Florida voted overwhelmingly for statehood; West Florida produced a slight majority in favor of the step; and East Florida cast its vote overwhelmingly against the move.[25] Despite the rather obvious regional differences, a majority supported statehood and the governor issued a call for a constitutional convention which would meet in December of the following year. In the meantime, to strengthen his position as well as to provide a basis

23. St. Augustine *Florida Herald*, December 1, 1836.
24. *Ibid.*, May 5, 1838.
25. Dorothy Dodd, *Florida Becomes a State* (Tallahassee, 1945), pp. 34, 37-38.

for representation in the newly organized upper house of the Legislative Council, Call ordered a territorial census.[26]

Regardless of these preparations, the ultimate decision regarding statehood, and especially its timing, remained largely a congressional matter. Yet internally these initial steps precipitated disruptive forces which neither Call nor his supporters in the Nucleus foresaw. Other factors aggravated the situation. The freeze of 1835 caused serious financial damage to the citrus growers of East Florida. The Seminole War was a nerve-racking and deadly affair for much of Florida, particularly for those along the extended frontier of East Florida. And then, on the heels of the statehood referendum, came the Panic of 1837. Florida's early banking system, barely under way, was dealt a heavy blow from which it never really recovered. On May 10 New York banks suspended specie payments. Baltimore, Philadelphia, and Boston institutions adopted similar measures. By June Florida banks had followed suit.[27] Sizeable federal expenditures during the Indian conflict temporarily bolstered a sagging economy, but the key issue had been found which would finally crystallize territorial factions. The "Bank"—the monster, the monopoly, the seat of aristocracy, the basis of power, the cause of privilege—became the focus of attack and its destruction the symbol of a new movement. East Florida and segments of the other two regions had opposed statehood. But they found in the election for convention delegates, the convention itself, and the drafting of a proposed state constitution not only means of attacking the banking institutions, but also opportunity to undermine the existing power structure.

Middle Florida, home of the Union Bank, large plantation center, and locus of political influence, sought to minimize factionalism, particularly with respect to the bank. Others would have it otherwise, especially in East Florida. James M. Gould, influential editor of the St. Augustine *Florida Herald*, invoked Clio in his pursuit of perspective and party. "Where," he asked, "are our Political Land-Marks?" They were embodied in the *struggles* of the past, he concluded, in the *conflicts* among Adams, Hamilton, and Jefferson, in the great debate between the Democrats and the Federalists. But "How do matters stand now?" he inquired. "Where are our great political leaders? And where is the democracy and who are they?"[28]

26. A bicameral Council replaced the single chamber in 1838.—Martin, *Territorial Days*, pp. 38-39.

27. Pensacola *Gazette*, May 13, June 10, 1837.      28. April 28, 1838.

Mr. Gould was raising a lot of relevant questions. The answers would soon be forthcoming. Moreover, he would contribute to their coming, not the least by virtue of his having called for them in the first place. To accusations that he and like-minded souls were local specimens of "locofocoism," he pleaded guilty and insisted that the time had come when people faced the necessity of looking "to principles, not men."[29]

The present paucity of materials makes it difficult to pinpoint the exact time of this political eruption. It is clear, however, that by July, 1838, Florida's "era of good feelings" had come to an end. Office seekers for the Legislative Council and the constitutional convention were beginning to define their positions a bit more clearly—even a bit more carefully. The territorial press, with few exceptions, emerged loudly and defiantly from their shells of neutrality. Across the entire territory, from the Jacksonville *Courier* to the Pensacola *Gazette,* Florida editors hurled invective at each other and their respective opponents with increasing alacrity.

The fall elections for the Legislative Council that year received more than the usual public attention because of the simultaneous selection of delegates to the constitutional convention.[30] To the entire brew was also added the potent stimulant of partisan politics. Party names and organizations did not exist as yet, though platforms upon which candidates stood did begin to emerge. Still, party lines were by no means clearly drawn and some individuals were not always readily classified. The example of Duval County's Isaiah D. Hart was by no means unusual. Though endorsed as a candidate for the territorial Senate by a group of "aroused citizens" of East Florida, he would also, by 1840, be the "Whig candidate" for the same post.[31] Nevertheless, the voters were presented with a more clearly cut picture of the issues, albeit with a partisan perspective.

In East Florida's leading community of St. Augustine a group of "Democratic Republican Citizens" placed advertisements in the *Florida Herald* attacking speculators and moneyed institutions. They called for a vote based upon principles and presented their list of properly principled candidates for the convention—Robert Raymond Reid, David Levy, Joseph S. Sanchez, and Edwin T. Jenckes. For

29. June 16, October 6, 1838.
30. J. P. DuVal, *Compilation of Legislative Acts* (Tallahassee, 1839), p. 433.
31. St. Augustine *Florida Herald,* October 13, 1838; Tallahassee *Floridian,* October 31, 1840.

9

the St. Johns County representatives in the Council they supported Jenckes and Elias B. Gould. As East Florida's first senators they favored Levy of St. Johns County, Hart of Duval County, and Francis R. Sanchez of Alachua County.[32] What is especially significant here is that, aside from Hart, these men were to constitute much of the inner core of the emerging Democratic party of East Florida. Similar developments took place in Middle and West Florida, where local slates, put forth by rebellious groups, provided victorious candidates who would also serve as future party leaders in the respective areas.

As the campaign progressed, the financial institutions served more and more as the overriding issue, for on the outcome hinged key decisions of the convention and with it the probable fate of those banks.[33] Consequently, the bank and antibank forces marshaled their supporters in a campaign of unprecedented excitement.[34] The pitch would become more feverish in the campaigns ahead, but for the present something new obviously had been added to the political scene. In the frontier east the *Florida Herald*, sensing the rising tide, added the words *Southern Democrat* to its name and launched its career as the leading party organ of that region.[35] It should be noted too that in concentrating their attack on the bank and thus obscuring other issues of the day, East Floridians not only elected antibank men, but antibank men who were, by and large, also in favor of statehood!

The delegates to Florida's first constitutional convention gathered in St. Joseph on the first Monday in December, 1838. When the Legislative Council selected that community as the seat of deliberation, it had aroused considerable consternation among the merchants and residents of nearby Apalachicola.[36] The brief history of St. Joseph, created in 1835 and incorporated the following year, well illustrates the pathetic experience of frontier settlement, town speculation, brief business boom, collapse, and disappearance.[37] But late in 1838 as convention delegates from all over the sprawling territory poured into the lively town, seizing beds wherever availa-

32. St. Augustine *Florida Herald*, October 6, 1838.
33. F. W. Hoskins, "The St. Joseph Convention," *Florida Historical Quarterly*, XVI (October, 1937), 107.
34. Tallahassee *Floridian*, November 3, 1838.
35. November 8, 1838 (name unchanged for citation herein).
36. Apalachicola *Gazette*, February 19, 1838.
37. Knauss, "St. Joseph: An Episode of the Economic and Political History of Florida," *Florida Historical Quarterly*, V (April, 1927), 181, 184; Carter, *Florida Territory*, pp. 639-41.

ble and taxing the facilities of the local bars, St. Joe was still in its ascendancy. Among the new dissidents from St. Augustine came Reid and Levy, both of whom would play a strategic role in the convention and in the formative party period which followed.

Robert Raymond Reid, born on September 8, 1789, was admitted to the Georgia bar and served with distinction as judge of the Superior Court in Augusta during the 1820's. Apparently he served too well, for the local forces finally managed to dispose of him by sending him to Washington as congressman.[38] In 1832 he was appointed United States Judge for East Florida, where he continued to hold court until 1839.[39] When President Van Buren removed Richard Call in that year, Reid moved on to the position of territorial governor.

Among the young lawyers trained in Judge Reid's St. Augustine office was David Levy. Born June 2, 1810, on the Danish island of St. Thomas, he was brought by his father Moses Elias Levy to Norfolk, Virginia, in 1819. There he attended a private school until 1827 and then moved to Alachua County, Florida, where he lived and worked on his father's sugar plantation. Sometime in 1830 or 1831 he moved again, this time to St. Augustine, and applied himself to the business of the law, completing his studies with Reid after the latter's arrival in 1832.[40] Levy rapidly made a name for himself and was elected to the 1837 Legislative Council. His industry, legal talents, ability in debate, and intellectual acumen were locally acclaimed and he was re-elected to the 1838 session.[41]

Among the Middle Florida delegates to the convention James D. Westcott, Jr., soon led the pack. He was born in Virginia, lived a few years in New Jersey where he was admitted to the bar, and in 1829 was appointed to a position in the consular bureau in Washington. Later he served briefly as secretary of the Florida territory.[42] No leader of major territorial status came from the West Florida contingent, though Walker Anderson was probably one of the more

38. Lester B. Shippee (ed.), *Bishop Whipple's Southern Diary, 1843-1844* (Minneapolis, 1937), p. 46.

39. Stephen F. Miller, *The Bench and Bar in Georgia* (2 vols.; Philadelphia, 1858), II, 235-36.

40. Arthur W. Thompson, "David L. Yulee: A Study of Nineteenth Century American Thought and Enterprise" (Ph.D. dissertation, Columbia University, 1954), pp. 6-8. Levy adopted the ancestral patronymic of Yulee in 1845 and from that point on was known as David L(evy) Yulee.

41. *Ibid.*; Pensacola *Gazette*, February 11, 1837.

42. Rerick, *Memoirs of Florida*, II, 214.

11

prominent. He, too, was born in Virginia and studied law. In 1831 he became professor of history and English literature at the University of North Carolina, and in 1835 migrated to Pensacola where he began his legal career.[43]

When the convention was called to order on December 3, 1838, the first major order of business was the election of a presiding officer. Robert Reid's victory over former Governor William P. Du-Val, the Union Bank attorney, by the narrow vote of 27 to 26 reflected the bitter campaign that had preceded it. It underscored too the impressive victory by the antibank forces during the course of that year. Almost immediately one of Reid's votes was challenged on a technicality. Though it was probably a valid ballot, because of his one-vote margin of victory Reid declared the chair vacant. DuVal, either because he recognized what the ultimate result would be anyway or because he hoped to calm the antibank storm, nominated Reid who was promptly re-elected unanimously.[44]

The East Florida old guard, however, was still dissatisfied. Peter Sken Smith, closely tied to the Southern Life Insurance and Trust Company and director of a number of proposed transportation schemes,[45] had lost the election for convention delegate to David Levy by only 24 votes.[46] He and his supporters then decided that Mr. Levy was an alien whose victory should be contested. "Judge Reid," it was bitterly contended, "was elected by *one* vote . . . that vote was an *alien's*."[47] The issue stemmed from a disagreement as to whether or not Levy's father had in fact actually been *in* St. Augustine by July 17, 1821, the date fixed by Governor Jackson to determine the inhabitants' eligibility for citizenship. Smith's move failed, but the technicality would continue to plague Levy's political career for nearly a decade.[48]

After the selection of a president, the convention turned to the real task at hand. Reid's suggestion that their job was too important

43. *Ibid.*, 86.

44. *Journal of the Proceedings of a Convention of Delegates to Form a Constitution for the People of Florida, held at St. Joseph, December, 1838* (St. Joseph, 1839), p. 15. Hereafter cited as *Convention Journal*.

45. St. Johns and St. Augustine Canal Company, Florida Peninsula Railroad and Steamboat Company, and St. Augustine and Picolata Railroad Company.

46. St. Augustine *News,* February 16, 1839.

47. *Ibid.*, December 22, 1838.

48. The issue in 1838 was settled by the territorial courts and in 1841 the contested delegate election by the U. S. House of Representatives; both decisions were in Levy's favor. The 1845 debate was never brought before the U. S. Senate.—Thompson, p. 24.

to permit the interference of partisan politics may have been a momentary emotional lapse following his election as presiding officer;[49] but whether intended or not, his expressed wish went largely unfulfilled. One of the early manifestations of partisan debate came in the drafting of the "Declaration of Rights." On the general principles of popular sovereignty, the social compact, the "natural and inalienable rights" of free speech, press, assembly, petition, and due process—the broad concensus which American culture had achieved by this stage of its history—there was no disagreement.[50] But matters relating to religious tests as well as to voting did cause some commotion. John L. McKinnon, to be Walton County Whig representative from 1840 to 1842, proposed that "No person who denies the being of a God, or a future state of rewards and punishments, shall hold any office in the civil department of this state." His proposal was promptly rejected by a vote of 36 to 18.[51]

Colonel Abram Bellamy, soon to become a Jefferson County Democratic leader, countered with the move that no minister of the gospel should be eligible for governor or membership in either house of the General Assembly. It was carried 29 to 27, though not by a clear-cut party division.[52] Levy's suggestion to disfranchise any party to a duel did not carry, though Leigh Read, later a participant in a highly controversial affair with political overtones, voted *for* the motion.[53]

The real battle, of course, came on the matter of banking. Despite repeated efforts on the part of several delegates to reach the controversial issue, and numerous resolutions obviously designed to bring the smoldering question to the floor, a group led by President Reid managed to postpone the inevitable clash. Through much of December procrastination was the order of the day, at least until enough of the constitution could be written to discourage any permanent breakdown. After Christmas Thomas Baltzell, prominent Leon County leader and Democratic candidate for the territorial Senate in 1842 and 1844, promoted a preliminary skirmish by denouncing the "improvident legislation of the Territorial Government" which created banking corporations "with unusual and extraordinary powers, to the obvious detriment of the public." The national government, he argued, had power over the territory and

49. *Convention Journal*, p. 6.
50. *Constitution or Form of Government for the People of Florida* (Tallahassee, 1851), Article I.   51. *Convention Journal*, p. 57.
52. *Ibid.*, p. 58.   53. *Ibid.*, p. 57.

13

should protect the people by repealing those charters. Colonel William H. Wyatt, Leon County Whig-to-be, countered by suggesting that the purpose of the convention was to draft a future constitution, not to evaluate past performances. Another leading bank "Whig," Thomas Brown, argued in the same vein.[54]

Shortly thereafter the irrepressible revolt erupted on another front. David Levy's proposal that "all lands liable to taxation in the State shall be taxed in proportion to their value" was carried 25 to 21 on the basis of a fairly clear party division.[55] The temper of the "Democrats" and the probable decision of the convention on the banks became perfectly clear. The conservatives lost all patience and unleashed the full fury of their attack. Denouncing the anti-bank men as "Levellers" and "Destructives," the bank party held a secret caucus and discussed appropriate strategy. Some actually suggested that they make an effort to break up the convention. The proposal apparently leaked out and an irate member of the opposition broke into the session and denounced the plan.[56] The bank forces then decided to stand firm and try to weather the storm.

By the end of the month the report of the banking committee was finally brought to the floor. James D. Westcott, Jr., had served as chairman, and together with other members of the committee, including David Levy, he produced a document thoroughly distasteful to the bank forces. Resolving itself into a committee of the whole, the convention braced itself for the clash which finally came in the first week of the new year. Wyatt's motion in defense of limited liability was defeated 30 to 21.[57] East Florida's Edwin T. Jenckes argued that the General Assembly should not pledge the faith and credit of the state to raise funds in support of any corporation. His move was carried 31 to 21.[58] Wyatt returned and, in defense of past Union Bank practices, moved that bank charters contain no restriction on raising money based upon real and personal property pledges. This was defeated by a vote of 26 to 19.[59] Baltzell then formalized his earlier expressions by urging that the President and both houses of Congress be asked to take appropriate action to protect the people of Florida from further banking mischief. It carried 29 to 26.[60] Dade County's Richard Fitzpatrick

54. *Ibid.*, pp. 59-61, 71. Wyatt ran unsuccessfully against Delegate James M. White in 1829, 1835, and 1837.    55. *Ibid.*, p. 64.
56. St. Augustine *Florida Herald*, September 12, 1840.
57. *Convention Journal*, p. 75.
58. *Ibid.*, p. 76.    59. *Ibid.*, p. 77.    60. *Ibid.*, pp. 85-86.

14

provided some comedy relief by moving that further discussion on the bank question be postponed until the Fourth of July.

Motions, substitute motions, amendments, and roll calls continued to be brought up for over a week. Finally, on Wednesday, January 9, Article XIII—Banks and other Corporations—was adopted, with the antibank position being carried 35 to 19. The triumph was confirmed the next day when a motion to reconsider lost and the article again passed, this time by 37 to 18.[61]

Article XIII was a sweeping indictment of the territorial banking system and a repudiation of the economic tactics of the Nucleus. Various sections provided for: a two-thirds vote of each house of the General Assembly to incorporate; a minimum of twenty individuals for a bank charter, a majority of whom had to be residents of the state; the exclusion of banking corporations from speculation or dealings in real estate, stock in other corporations, chattels, merchandise, insurance, manufacturing, etc.; a minimum of $100,000 capitalization for banks based upon "actual payment of specie therein" and a prohibition against any borrowing to create that capital; a maximum profit of 10 per cent; a restriction that a bank's stockholders "shall be individually, and severally liable for the payment of all of its debts, in proportion to the stock owned by each"; quarterly statements to the governor; annual inspection by the state; and the fact that "The General Assembly shall not pledge the faith and credit of the State, to raise funds in aid of any corporation whatsoever."[62] It was manifestly a triumph for the antibank forces and a manifesto for the emerging Jacksonian Democrats.

In analyzing the convention journal, it is clear that the new "Democratic" leaders did not vote as a bloc on all issues. Questions such as boundaries, representation, location of the capital, among others, revealed personal, local, sectional, and other divergencies which frequently ran counter to party affiliation. But on subjects of taxation and banking corporations, the pending party division became apparent. In vote after vote hitherto cited on these two topics, the delineation of opposing factions was most evident. It remained for the leaders of the new force to effect some kind of organization through which they could minimize their differences, consolidate their position, mobilize their following, and translate their will into continuing political action.

61. *Ibid.*, pp. 112-14.
62. *Constitution . . . for the People of Florida*, Article XIII.

With the adjournment of the convention and before the departure of the Democrats from St. Joseph, the initial step was taken. On Saturday evening, January 11, 1839, a Florida Democratic Republican meeting was held at Captain Simmons' Hotel. Convention delegates were joined by visiting sympathizers.[63] Walker Anderson, future chief justice of the State Supreme Court, was elected president. Three vice-presidents representing East, Middle, and West Florida were also selected: Edwin T. Jenckes of St. Johns County, Abram Bellamy of Jefferson County, and Gabriel J. Floyd of Calhoun County. Dr. Edward R. Gibson of St. Joseph and Buckingham Smith of St. Augustine served as secretaries. James D. Westcott, Jr., addressed the conclave and presented a lengthy resolution, probably prepared jointly with Leigh Read, J. N. Partridge, Joseph McCants, Gibson, and Levy. After some discussion it was adopted unanimously. The resolution deprecated "the personal excitements, not originating in principle, which have heretofore characterized the political contests in Florida." It demanded that all candidates provide "a full, unambiguous, and public declaration of their opinions, views, and principles on all subjects of public interests." It applauded the leading measures of the Van Buren administration and paid homage to Andrew Jackson.[64] It denounced "abolition incendiarism." It agreed to effect some kind of organization "so necessary in all political contests, to ensure the triumph of correct principles." And, finally, it provided for concrete party organization through the selection of county committees of correspondence and a central committee in Tallahassee.[65] Fully satisfied with their constitutional labors and party liaisons in St. Joseph, the Democratic leaders departed for their homes and the next phase of their movement. The party strife of the Jackson era had taken hold belatedly on the Florida frontier.

63. St. Augustine *News*, February 23, 1839.
64. Reference to Jackson was not by name, but as "that distinguished statesman of the South. . . ." It is conceivable that they had Calhoun in mind, though the context points to the former President. It is also possible that the omission of the name was a fence-straddling device.
65. St. Augustine *Florida Herald*, February 21, 1839.

# 2. SWEEP TO POWER

The election of a territorial delegate to Congress in the spring of 1839 provided the Florida Democrats with their first opportunity for partisan activity since the St. Joseph convention. The results were not altogether encouraging. To begin with, no political label could readily be pinned on the incumbent Charles Downing. Joseph M. White, after twelve years of service, had retired in 1837 and East Florida's Downing became his successor. He did so largely because there were two candidates from Middle Florida—William H. Wyatt, soon to become an antibank Whig, and Leigh Read, similarly an antibank Democrat. The problem in 1839 was that many Floridians were still not sure in which political camp Downing would come to rest. Though close to the St. Augustine bank and tied to the conservative group in Florida, he was called a Democrat in Washington. On the other hand, in some financial circles outside the territory he was already referred to as a Whig.[1] To complicate matters, his opponent in 1839, Thomas Baltzell of Leon County, though a Democrat, was occasionally labeled a Whig. Nor, it should be added, were all East Florida Democrats convinced that Baltzell was really in the antibank camp.[2] Party affiliations of the candidates, then, were obscure. Partisan division was further blurred by the simultaneous vote on the issue of accepting or rejecting the proposed state constitution. Here sectional differences cut across party lines and the outcome was probably a better reflection of the popular outlook on statehood than of party strength.[3] Downing won by at least a 600-vote majority, his greatest strength coming from strongly antistatehood East Florida. The proponents of the constitution were victorious by the barest of margins, a majority of their votes coming from Middle Florida.[4]

By the fall election for the Legislative Council that year the Democrats had progressed further in their organization and were

1. Charleston *Mercury*, June 4, 1838, quoted in St. Augustine *Florida Herald*, June 16, 1838.

2. St. Augustine *News*, May 11, 1839. Baltzell also lost votes because many in East Florida were disappointed in the number of legislative seats given that area in the proposed constitution.—Dodd, *Florida Becomes a State*, pp. 60, 320-21.

3. The statehood question will be discussed in Chap. 3.

4. See Table 3.

far more successful in their drive for power.[5] As party lines became more sharply drawn, a number of candidates engaged in the inevitable backtracking. In St. Johns County, for example, Benjamin A. Putnam had the usual conservative and bank support. But in seeking to win the endorsement of the Democratic party, he flatly announced that he had not voted for the Southern Life Insurance and Trust Company charter and pledged his support for the attack against it. The unhappy fact is that Mr. Putnam had indeed voted for the charter in 1835; moreover, he did not join the attack in 1840.[6]

During what was really the first partisan campaign for the Council, the assertions of the Democrats aroused both concern and scorn among the opposition. In East Florida, for example, the Democrats were referred to as the "Jeffersonian Humbuggists." The sincerity of their opposition to statehood as well as their support for "division"—which would have created an independent East Florida Territory—was challenged. The anti-Democratic St. Augustine *News* accused them of favoring division, "but it is a *division of the loaves and fishes.*"[7] In West Florida the cry was essentially the same. There they were denounced as "The Sans Culotte Party . . . *alias* the Florida Jeffersonian Democratic Republican anti-Bank, agrarian Party."[8]

There were other views too. One self-styled "poor man" bluntly indicated that what he and people like him needed was a little hard cash.[9] Whatever else was involved, this disgruntled individual had put his finger on the basic issue. By general concensus, the Democratic attack on the bank "ragocracy" was the key to the election of 1839.[10] Indeed, the anti-Democratic St. Joseph *Times*, correctly predicting the Democratic victory, suggested that "If the Banks had paid specie or parted with exchange at par, such would not have been the result."[11] In East Florida the Democrats captured six of the eleven seats, winning five of the nine counties, losing two, and splitting one. The triumph was even greater in Middle Florida

5. The fall election which usually took place in early October was for the selection of members of the Legislative Council which would convene the following January.

6. *Legislative Council Journal* (1835), pp. 65, 68.

7. October 11, 1839.

8. St. Joseph *Times,* October 1, 1839.

9. Apalachicola *Courier,* October 15, 1839.

10. Apalachicola *Gazette,* September 4, 1839.

11. October 1, 1839.

18

where the Democrats swept eight of the ten seats, gaining control of three of the five counties, while losing only one and splitting another. In West Florida they garnered five—and possibly six—of the eight seats, while winning three counties, losing two and producing at least a split in another.[12]

The fall election of 1840 gave the Democratic cause further impetus. In addition to the annual scramble for the territorial House, the biennial canvass for the Senate added to the number of candidates as well as to the excitement. In the upper body the Democrats increased their number by winning all four of the East Florida senatorial seats, though losing the seven Middle and West Florida vacancies. The enlarged Democratic minority, along with a group of antibank Whigs, however, could control the basic issue of the day. In the lower house they retained their commanding majority, scoring a complete sweep of every seat and every county in frontier East Florida. Their earlier Middle and West Florida majorities were cut to maximum minorities. Still, they continued to hold nineteen of the House's twenty-nine seats.[13]

The Democratic victories continued for still another year. In 1841 the party came up with approximately twenty of the twenty-nine House seats, capturing nine of East Florida's eleven seats, seven of Middle Florida's ten, and four or five of West Florida's eight.[14] Moreover, in a special Middle Florida Senate contest to replace William P. DuVal who had resigned, Democrat James A. Berthelot defeated the Conservative candidate Leslie A. Thompson "by a large majority." Municipal victories added depth to the Democratic strength. In St. Augustine, for example, Elias B. Gould defeated the former Whig representative Benjamin A. Putnam for mayor; and all four of the aldermen also were Democrats.[15] The opposition was thoroughly discouraged, one paper conceding even before the election took place that the Whigs "stood about the same chance that a white man does with Indians."[16]

The Democratic successes in 1839, 1840, and 1841 gave them increasing control over the decisions of the Legislative Council sessions in 1840, 1841, and 1842, but there were two other facets to

12. See Table 2.
13. See tables 1 and 2. To eliminate unnecessary confusion, South Florida's tallies are included with East Florida's.
14. The inconclusive totals occur because a few candidates cannot be classified politically. See Table 2.
15. St. Augustine *Florida Herald*, November 1, 1841.
16. St. Augustine *News*, October 15, 1841.

19

their sweep to territorial power. One was control of the governor's office, the other the delegate to Congress. Richard Keith Call, leader of the Nucleus and Florida's most prominent Whig in the forties, was still governor. His break with Jackson had been followed by a complete rupture with Van Buren and the Democrats in the late thirties. Frustrated in his military ambitions, Call was something less than circumspect in his criticism of the War Department's handling of the Seminole War. Though some of the governor's comments were probably well taken, Joel R. Poinsett, Secretary of War and Van Buren intimate, was irked. It took little persuasion from the Florida Democrats, therefore, to effect Call's removal. In his place the President appointed Robert Raymond Reid on December 13, 1839.[17] Earlier efforts to discredit Reid on the grounds of political partisanship while a judge, which would block his selection, had failed.[18] To work with Reid, Joseph McCants, Jefferson County Democrat, was appointed secretary of the territory.[19] By 1840, then, the Democrats had gained control of the legislative and executive branches of the territorial government. There remained only the matter of congressional delegate.

Charles Downing, who had been re-elected in 1839, had proved more and more of a disappointment to the Democrats, and by 1841 they were ready with their own candidate—David Levy. That Levy was already the choice of many party leaders in 1840 is quite evident. To begin with, Reid and other ranking Democrats had sent Levy to Washington the year before to confer with the President. One objective of the Washington visit was to undermine the influence of Downing, who by that time had clearly swung into the Whig camp.[20] Moreover, though virtually assured of victory in a Democratic bull electorate, Levy had declined an East Florida convention's nomination for the territorial Senate in the fall of 1840.[21]

17. M. Van Buren to J. Forsyth, December 13, 1839 (Records of the States of the United States: A Microfilm Compilation, Florida, E. 2). To Poinsett's letter of November 29, 1839, requesting Call's removal the President noted, "Let Gov. Call be superseded & Judge Reed [sic] appointed in his place."— Carter, Florida Territory, pp. 656-67.

18. St. Augustine News, December 27, 1839; W. G. Fouraker, "The Administration of Robert Raymond Reid" (Master's thesis, Florida State University, 1949), p. 7.

19. M. Van Buren to A. Vail, November 15, 1839 (Microfilm Records of the States, Florida, E. 2).

20. R. R. Reid to M. Van Buren, March 5, 1840 (Van Buren Papers, Library of Congress); Thompson, "David L. Yulee," p. 21.

21. St. Augustine Florida Herald, September 27, 1840.

20

Early in 1841 his time had come. At a meeting of delegates from the different districts of Florida David Levy was nominated as the Democratic party's candidate for delegate. Endorsed as an industrious, faithful, intelligent, and honest individual, as a man of integrity, and, as always, a candidate of the people—it was enough to give any human a real glow.[22]

George T. Ward, the Whig candidate from Middle Florida, favored statehood, opposed division of the territory, and stood foursquare for the existing bank system. Indeed, Ward had not only introduced the Union Bank Bill in 1833, he was also a substantial stockholder and since 1835 a director. There was no question where he stood! Downing, refusing to be brushed aside, joined the campaign. He opposed statehood, more or less favored division, but also, like Ward, supported the banks—associated as he had been with the St. Augustine institution.[23]

Levy and the Democrats cleverly ignored both the statehood and division questions and concentrated their fire against the banks. By so doing, they were able to unite the assorted antibank groups from all parts of Florida, regardless of regional differences on the other two issues. This, moreover, coupled with the fact that the Whig opposition was split in Florida as in earlier campaigns in other parts of the nation, particularly New York and Virginia, contributed to another Democratic victory.[24] By securing more votes in East Florida than his two opponents combined, and by winning as many votes in Middle Florida as Ward, Levy captured the delegate's post as a plurality victor, some 500 votes short of a majority.[25] In an open letter to the public Levy urged "that my services be freely commanded by all who have occasion for them" and then departed for the nation's capital.[26] Downing followed and contested the election in the House of Representatives on the citizenship issue. Ward, in a less contentious mood, decided "to visit Saratoga, drink its sparkling waters, [and] gaze at the pretty women there."[27]

By May, 1841, therefore, the Democrats had achieved their triple victory. They had a commanding majority in the lower house of the

22. Tallahassee *Floridian*, February 20, 1841.
23. *Ibid.*, February 27, 1841; St. Augustine *Florida Herald*, April 2, 9, 1841.
24. Wilfred E. Binkley, *American Political Parties* (New York, 1945), p. 161; Thompson, "David L. Yulee," p. 23.
25. See Table 3.
26. St. Augustine *Florida Herald*, June 11, 1841; Tallahassee *Floridian*, June 26, 1841.                27. Tallahassee *Florida Sentinel*, June 7, 1841.

Legislative Council and had improved their position in the Senate; they had Reid and McCants as territorial governor and secretary; and now David Levy was on his way to Washington, both as delegate to Congress and as Democrat-in-residence. Though it was soon to be disrupted, the Jacksonian Democratic sweep to power was virtually complete.

# 3. PARTY ISSUES

In the summer of 1838 the Democratic party in Florida was non-existent, at best a gleam in the eyes of a few would-be leaders. In less than three years its reasonably well-oiled machine, utilizing a variety of locally untried tactics, had ridden to power. That there were those who sought political power for personal reasons, for status, or possibly even as an occupation cannot be denied. Still, the conflicts, the emotions, the debates which were stirred up in this period bespeak the existence of real issues. Some were of continuing national significance, such as the statehood question; some were the consequence of earlier expansionism and of the frontier process, such as the Seminole War; some were the result of both national *and* local developments, such as the future of the banking institutions; some stemmed from the general maturation of the region itself and the intraterritorial conflicts that this growth generated, such as the fights over division and sectional representation in the Legislative Council; some were derived from larger issues, such as the dispute over the militia which followed the Seminole War; others undoubtedly originated because of purely local disagreements; and still others spilled over in the general backwash of the Jackson movement with its drive for a more popular and responsive government. By 1840 each of them, directly or indirectly, touched the mass of Floridians. Different issues differently affected the three sections, the diverse elements of the social stratification, and the mass of citizens. The total number of responses, as well as the motivation for those responses, defy ready classification. Nonetheless, using the political institution—and particularly a series of successive elections—as a partial index of cultural change, it is possible to concentrate on a group of basic issues which moved a host of individuals and changed aspects of their society, in turn.

Undoubtedly the banks constituted the major issue of the late territorial period. To the general condemnation of the entire banking system which developed after 1838 was added specific opposition to the issuance of any further territorial-guaranteed bonds, as well as increasing accusations of mismanagement and excessive speculation.[1] As a consequence, a growing number of Floridians

1. Martin, *Florida During Territorial Days*, p. 151; Pensacola *Gazette*, September 9, 1837.

were involved in the political controversy which centered on the banks, quickly arraying themselves for or against the institutions. The strong antibank provisions of the proposed constitution not only reflected a segment of vocal territorial opinion, but also served to crystallize latent opposition against what was termed the "Shin-Plaster Nobility" together with its "banking . . . credit. . . American . . . protective . . . and all those other *systems* so well calculated to depress the industrious laboring classes. . . ."[2]

The bank had become more than a key issue; it was a symbol whose continued existence appeared to threaten the possibility of achieving broader political and economic change. There were those among the salaried groups, the growing number of petty entrepreneurs, and particularly the yeomen who took a dim view of the monetary situation. For many bewilderment or apathy was the initial reaction. But when the frontier farmer came to town to make some purchases or send a remittance, he discovered as one individual disgustedly reported in 1838: "I should lose about a bit in a dollar."[3] Middle Florida merchants began to complain that Union Bank bills had depreciated from 20 to 30 per cent below their nominal value. The probank St. Joseph *Times* warned, "It is felt by every man who buys a barrel of flour or the daily sustenance for which he labours."[4] Such occurrences quickly transformed apathy or bewilderment into overt bitterness and filled the Democratic ranks. Anger against the banks also came when individuals or small entrepreneurs who criticized the operations of the banks were subjected to public denunciation and economic pressure.[5] Democrats were quick to capitalize on these developments. David Levy uttered a typical comment of the time when he declared that the banks were a device of the privileged few for swindling the hard-working many.[6]

To the mounting criticism of the adverse economic influences of the banks was soon added an emotional element predicated on the belief that they had been largely responsible for the creation of an aristocracy. A widespread conviction grew that bank policies and tactics had created unjustified wealth, extravagance, and "sham

2. St. Augustine *Florida Herald*, March 5, July 17, 1840; Tallahassee *Floridian*, February 1, 1840.

3. This applied to the bills of the Southern Life Insurance and Trust Company.—St. Augustine *Florida Herald*, May 26, 1838.

4. April 1, 1840.

5. Pensacola *Gazette*, November 3, 1838.

6. D. Levy to the Editor, Tallahassee *Floridian*, August 1, 1840.

luxury."[7] Worse still was the feeling that the "three great banking monsters" were exercising disproportionate political power and influence in their respective areas of Florida.[8] For those still blind to the "obvious evils" of the banks, or those still deaf to the pleas of the Democrats, be they misguided Whigs or political nonparticipants, there was always the occasional invocation of sectionalism, nativism, and antisemitism. Who, after all, owned the bank bonds? To whom would the people's taxes go to pay the interest on those defaulted faith bonds? To *European* and *Northern* bankers! To the "Shylocks of Wall Street and their colleagues, the Jew Brokers of London."[9]

Despite the attack on the banks by the St. Joseph convention, Governor Richard Call defended the territorial financial institutions in his message of January 8, 1839, to the Legislative Council.[10] Thus, the governor accepted the Democratic challenge and the banks became the main issue in the fall Legislative Council campaigns from 1839 to 1842.[11]

Not all Whigs, however, were as willing as Call to join battle on the bank question. In the 1840 campaign the "States'-rights Whigs" led by William Wyatt were quite ready to ignore the item and allow the faith bonds to be in default. The "probank Whigs" under the banner of the Conservative party supported Call. During the following year's campaign the states' righters deviated even more by suggesting that the territorial banks were beyond salvation. They went so far as to argue that the governor and Council had no power to pledge the territory's faith.[12] The Conservatives continued their defense of the banks, though by this time they were evasive on the use of public funds to pay interest on bonds which were by then in default.[13] The Whig split, therefore, was a substantial factor in the Democratic victories.

7. Florida *Senate Journal* (1844), p. 72; St. Augustine *Florida Herald*, July 7, 1838.

8. J. Branch to M. Van Buren, February 5, 1839; A. Balch to M. Van Buren, April 3, 1840 (Van Buren Papers, Library of Congress).

9. Tallahassee *Florida Sentinel*, May 28, 1841; St. Augustine *Florida Herald*, September 27, 1840; Abbey, "The Union Bank," p. 219. The intersectional controversy would not assume significant proportions in the party battles of Florida until the later 1840's. Antisemitism, used on occasion by both parties, would not be a major issue.

10. *House Journal* (1839), pp. 6-7.

11. Abbey, "The Union Bank," p. 220.

12. Tallahassee *Florida Sentinel*, September 17, 1841.

13. Tallahassee *Star of Florida*, September 29, 1841.

Other factors also aided the Democratic attack on the banks. The aftermath of the Panic of 1837 was keenly felt in Florida by 1840. The economic depression prompted the calling of public meetings in various parts of the territory, and resolutions were adopted against payment of debts in specie.[14] At one meeting a group of Tallahassee merchants agreed not to accept Union Bank notes at par.[15] Again seeking to exploit this reaction, Democratic leaders called for large antibank majorities as a demonstration to Congress that the people of the territory opposed the use of taxes for the payment of interest on faith bonds.[16]

Led by David Levy, James D. Westcott, Jr., and Walker Anderson of East, Middle, and West Florida respectively, the Democrats raised their voices against the banking institutions. Governor Robert Raymond Reid added to the outcry and brought the issue to a head in 1840. Reid had never cared for the local banks. As early as 1833 he had written, "The passion for bank making . . . in the territory . . . must prove injurious to the general interests. . . . They favor monopoly, make aristocracy, and create slaves."[17] Some of his critics accused him of being a bank man, but this stemmed from a loan Reid made at the St. Augustine bank to "prevent a free Negro from being separated from his wife." To do so he mortgaged a lot and a slave which the bank, in turn, used to secure a faith bond.[18] Despite this, Reid's position was clear. In speeches and at public meetings he invariably opposed any bank which received special grants and other legislative favors.[19] The major blow came in his first message to the Legislative Council in 1840. It was triggered by President Van Buren, against whom the Florida Democrats had earlier exerted much pressure, and it initiated a train of events which would ultimately destroy the territorial banking system.

In his message to Congress on December 2, 1839, the President reminded the congressmen that their Act of 1836 provided that no territorial incorporated bank had the force of law unless approved by them. But, he added, "acts of a very exceptional character pre-

14. Fouraker, "Robert Raymond Reid," pp. 40-41.

15. Tallahassee *Floridian*, March 28, 1840.

16. D. Levy to Dr. Edward R. Gibson, July 8, 1841, in St. Augustine *Florida Herald*, September 17, 1841.

17. Reid, "Diary," January 31, 1833, quoted in Fouraker, "Robert Raymond Reid," p. 22.

18. R. R. Reid to J. Forsyth, July 26, 1840, in "Letterbook of R. R. Reid, January, 1840—April, 1841" (Florida State Library, Tallahassee).

19. Fouraker, "Robert Raymond Reid," p. 21.

viously passed by the legislature of Florida were suffered to remain in force, by virture of which bonds may be issued to a very large amount by those institutions upon the faith of the Territory." The interests involved, he continued "are of great importance, and the subject deserves your early and careful attention."[20] The Senate responded by resolving that the President secure additional information on the situation in Florida. Secretary of State John Forsyth, in turn, relayed the Senate request to Governor Reid who in 1840 placed the matter before the Territorial Council. In his January message Reid initiated the subject with a denunciation of "monied monopolies" and those who would betray the rights of the people. He continued with an attack on the Union Bank of Tallahassee, indicating that in Middle Florida "its promises to pay are held in some suspicion and its credit is impaired." Its currency, he insisted, had depreciated to a point of being almost valueless in East and West Florida. Having roundly condemned the banks, he then urged a legislative investigation of the entire system, particularly with regard to possible mismanagement. His followers were only too happy to oblige.[21]

It was generally assumed at first that the investigation would be a joint enterprise of both houses. But the Senate, still containing a heavy probank contingent, procrastinated. The overwhelmingly Democratic lower house used the delay to proceed on its own and without possible obstruction. When the Senate finally did move for a joint committee, the House rejected the idea on the grounds that its investigation was already underway.

Actually there were two House committees; the Judiciary Committee, chaired by Walker Anderson, looked into the matter of the validity of the faith bonds; the Banking Committee, under the chairmanship of Elias E. Blackburn, investigated the Union Bank. The lengthy reports which were submitted to the lower house and the governor did not always exemplify the impartiality and the absence of party spirit which Reid had called for. They did uncover a large amount of interesting information and much future political ammunition. There for interested readers was a complete list of all stockholders, how much each had borrowed from his own bank, and the extent of the collateral provided by each. The lists of directors, stockholders, and borrowers proved rather embarrassing to the

20. James D. Richardson, *A Compilation of the Messages and Papers of the Presidents* (10 vols.; Washington, 1899), III, 540, 591.
21. *House Journal* (1840), pp. 11-13.

27

Whig party, for they bore a remarkable similarity to the roster of the leaders and major supporters of that group.[22] Worse still, the investigators uncovered a number of questionable practices. Property values, for example, had been grossly overestimated in order to insure larger mortgages. Slaves had been shunted back and forth between plantations so that the temporarily larger number of slaves would provide increased security for larger borrowing.[23] Again, cleared lands were frequently not used except to increase the official average "available for cultivation," thereby increasing mortgages. The list of deeds and misdeeds was imposing indeed. Particularly damaging to the future of the banks, more so to the bondholders, was the report of the Judiciary Committee. After a closely reasoned presentation, the committee concluded that there was no legal basis for the chartering of banks with exclusive privileges and that pledges of the faith and credit of the people of Florida were null and void.[24]

While the House Democrats reveled, the Senate Whigs reviled the report as "dangerous" and "subversive to settled order of society."[25] But there was more to come. In addition to the House investigation of Tallahassee's Union Bank, the lower chamber adopted a resolution asking Governor Reid to appoint a special commission to look into the bank situation outside of the capital.[26] Reid readily complied by establishing three committees. One, a group of six led by Edwin T. Jenckes, was to check on the Southern Life Insurance and Trust Company in St. Augustine. Edward R. Gibson led three others in a survey of Union Bank and Life and Trust branches in Apalachicola and St. Joseph. Later, Walker Anderson headed a committee to probe the Bank of Pensacola in his own county.[27]

During the course of 1840 the various reports filtered back to Reid. In one instance it was noted that Peter Sken Smith, functioning as cashier of the Southern Life Insurance and Trust Company, flatly refused to cooperate, and no records were opened for inspection. From the opposite end of the territory Anderson reported that the Bank of Pensacola was in a state of "utter and hopeless insolven-

22. *Ibid.*, Appendix, pp. 27-104.
23. *Ibid.*; Thomas, "Banking in Florida," p. 23.
24. *House Journal* (1840), Appendix, pp. 16-17.
25. *Senate Journal* (1840), p. 126.
26. *House Journal* (1840), pp. 129-30.
27. R. R. Reid to E. T. Jenckes, March 10, 1840; R. R. Reid to E. R. Gibson, March 14, 1840, in "Letterbook of R. R. Reid."
28. Tallahassee *Floridian*, August 1, 1840; Fouraker, "Robert Raymond Reid," pp. 26, 39.

cy."[28] The three reports were not particularly illuminating but, along with the House discoveries, served as excellent political ammunition. As a consequence, and on the assumption that the next Council would act one way or another on the bank issue, the fall campaign was bitterly fought. Despite another Democratic House and an increased number of Democrats in the Senate, little was accomplished in the legislative session of 1841. With only eleven members in the upper chamber, only six senators could, and often did, block the governor's requests and appointments. It was especially frustrating, since he could count at least eighteen of the twenty-nine lower house members safely in the Democratic fold. Reid attempted to overcome this situation by arguing that a majority vote of both houses combined was all that was needed. Otherwise, he contended, "a majority of the Council may be defeated by a minority of the same body."[29] The Senate failed to follow his logic.[30]

The 1841 legislature, therefore, did little or nothing about the banks. But the events that occurred immediately after the session made some kind of action the following year almost inevitable. To begin with, $15,000 had come due on January 1, 1840, for interest on $500,000 worth of Pensacola faith bonds. Another $15,000 payment had also passed unnoticed in Florida six months later. As a result, the London agent of the Bank of the United States had honored the $30,000 European bondholder request and the bank's president, T. Dunlap, then passed the bill on to the governor on March 3, 1841.[31] Reid responded by indicating that he thought Dunlap had waited an unnecessarily long time. Moreover, he accused Dunlap of deliberately delaying his letter until after the legislature had adjourned.[32] But this was only the beginning. On May 11, 1841, Amsterdam's Hope and Company protested to the American Minister to the Netherlands the nonpayment of interest on other Florida faith bonds. Three days later the Ministry passed the tidings on to Secretary of State Daniel Webster for transmission to Reid. Similarly, on May 26 a group of London firms—Gowan and Marx; Onernd, Gurney and Company; Grayson and Company; Tomson, Hankey and Company; Cautts and Company; and Ewart Taylor and Company—protested to Henry J. Williams of Philadel-

29. *Senate Journal* (1841), p. 16.
30. *Ibid.*, p. 27.
31. Tallahassee *Floridian*, April 3, 1841; St. Augustine *Florida Herald*, April 16, 1841.
32. R. R. Reid to T. Dunlap, March 30, 1841 in "Letterbook of R. R. Reid."

phia. On June 14 their communiqué was again forwarded to Webster to be passed on to Reid.[33]

It became quite evident by the summer of 1841 that the territorial government was faced not only with a bill of several hundred thousand dollars, but also with the prospect of this bill becoming cumulatively larger in the years to come. The Democratic response was simple. To the banks they cried, "Put your hands into your pockets" and "keep the people from *taxation*."[34] But neither the banks nor public taxes would provide the necessary interest payments. The legislature in 1842 found a less expensive solution in the form of repudiation.

The victory of William Henry Harrison and the Whigs in 1840 had, in the meantime, resulted in Reid's removal and Richard K. Call's re-appointment as governor of the territory. Despite the pleasure of his return, Call found himself in a rather difficult position. In his message of January 6, 1842, he rejected the idea of repudiation. On the other hand, another overwhelmingly Democratic House and widespread public opposition to increased taxation to salvage the banks directed his attention away from any immediate request for territorial payment. He suggested, instead, that the bondholders exhaust all legal steps against the banks before coming to the government. The Council was moving toward a more definite solution.

The House Committee on Corporations, chaired by Jefferson County's Democratic leader Elias E. Blackburn, unearthed additional testimony against the banks. Particularly damaging was the statement of John P. DuVal, former secretary of the territory, who swore that contrary to law he had not personally affixed the territorial seal or signed any of the $2,000,000 of Union Bank bonds.

I recollect [he stated] when entering my office one morning, I observed many pieces of circular papers on the floor, and enquired of Mr. Copeland, the Private Secretary of Governor Call, what he had been doing with them. He informed me, that the Governor and others had been executing the Territorial Bonds on account of the Union Bank during the previous night. I expressed my astonishment, as I had not been requested to affix the Seal of the Territory to the Bonds, nor had any intimation of the intention of the Governor to execute the Bonds.

I was afterwards informed that my office had been occupied until one or two o'clock at night by the Governor and others executing the Bonds. The Bank officers were in the habit of affixing the Ter-

33. St. Augustine *Florida Herald*, August 6, 1841.    34. *Ibid.*

ritorial Seal by permission of the Governor. On one occasion I called with one of the Bank officers, Mr. Rutgers, for the Seal at his house, and obtained it. Governor Call at one time gave orders to his Private Secretary to lock up the Territorial Seal so as to prevent its being in my custody.[35]

The antibank attack had reached flood tide; the Democrats were ready for action. In both houses they were joined by a minority Whig bloc which was apprehensive of Call's stand politically, on the one hand, and feared the possibility of being held personally liable, on the other hand. This coalition adopted a series of three bills which sought "to secure the people of Florida from the evils of a depreciated currency," to close the Union Bank for insolvency, and in effect to repudiate the faith bonds.[36] The action was too much for Call, who denounced the bills as "partial, illiberal and oppressive legislation." In vetoing all the proposals, he insisted that they attempted nothing less than "the utter annihilation of the banking institutions of the Territory." He argued further not only that the bank charters had created certain inviolable rights, but that they were also "sacred instrument[s]" whose "mantle covers with equal protection every person of this community, whether considered as an individual or as a member of a corporation."[37] James D. Westcott, Jr., joined Elias E. Blackburn and several other Democrats in a critique of Call's action; then both houses promptly passed all three bills over the governor's veto.[38]

The legislative repudiation of 1842 stood for the duration of the territorial era. And while the validity of repudiating the faith bonds was never finally established, neither was anything ever paid to the bondholders. Certainly Floridians were not going to tax themselves to pay northerners and foreigners. Debate on the issue continued sporadically, with a few insisting that they would never repudiate.[39] But with statehood in 1845 and the enforcement of the St. Joseph constitution, which prohibited taxation for any purpose other than necessary state expenses, the entire banking and faith bond question came to an end.

The Democrats had emerged triumphant on the major issue of the late territorial period, but there were other conflicts which

35. *House Journal* (1842), pp. 127-28.
36. *Ibid.*, pp. 172-74.   37. *Ibid.*, pp. 257-58, 260.
38. *Ibid.*, pp. 279-85, 297, 308; *Acts and Resolutions of the Legislative Council* (1842), pp. 45, 53.
39. Apalachicola *Commercial Advertiser*, May 4, 1844.

31

widened the breach between the parties and at the same time offered them opportunities for political advancement. One of the more significant was the problem of successfully terminating the protracted Seminole War, together with the controversy which centered on the Florida volunteer militia. To many, the banks and the Indians constituted a double-barreled menace. "Democrats of East Florida," they were warned, "keep a bright look out. Your opponents are as wiley as the Seminoles, and as faithless. The one would take your life—the other your liberty."[40]

Many of the Seminoles, remnants of the "Five Civilized Tribes," had avoided deportation to the Indian Territory, now Oklahoma. Instead they fled south into another American territory, but there too they faced the ever-advancing farmer and were "driven deeper and deeper into peninsular Florida."[41] The war began in 1835, when most of the Seminoles in Florida refused to accept the decision of some tribal chiefs to move westward, and a group under Osceola murdered a government agent.[42] Sometimes taking the offensive, the Indians carried out attacks in various parts of Alachua County and even in northern sections of the peninsula. Settlers soon deserted their homes and escaped to more settled communities, including St. Augustine and Tallahassee.[43] Others were less fortunate. Homes were burned; money and possessions were stolen; slaves were freed, kidnapped, and, if they resisted, butchered; itinerant ministers were murdered; settlers were terrorized, attacked, and many of them killed.[44]

Peace treaties and pacification attempts failed and the mutual hostility, barbarity, and killing continued. Ethan Allen Hitchcock, later a general, wrote his brother in 1840: "Five years ago I came as a volunteer, willingly making every effort in my power to be of service in punishing, as I thought, the Indians. I now come, with the persuasion that the Indians have been wronged and I enter upon one of the most hopeless tasks that was ever given to man to

40. St. Augustine *Florida Herald*, September 27, 1840.
41. John Collier, *Indians of the Americas* (New York, 1948), p. 125; Patrick, *Florida Under Five Flags*, p. 34.
42. Patrick, p. 34.
43. R. K. Call to John Warren, "Call Letterbook, 1836" (Florida Historical Society Library); *Bishop Whipple's Southern Diary*, pp. 70-71.
44. J. Garrason to R. R. Reid, March 18, 1840 (Historical Society of Pennsylvania); *Kendall's Expositor* (Washington), February 17, 1841; John T. Sprague, *The Origin, Progress and Conclusion of the Florida War* (New York, 1847), p. 232; Tallahassee *Floridian*, January 15, 1840; St. Augustine *Florida Herald*, November 15, 1839.

32

perform."[45] The yeomanry and the frontiersmen of East Florida were far less charitable in their sentiments toward the Indians. The repeated failures of Winfield Scott, Thomas Jesup, and Zachary Taylor also did little to ease their overt hostility either toward the army or toward the territorial government. But Robert Raymond Reid's appointment as governor in 1839 gave them new hope. This East Florida Democratic leader would surely do something! Almost at once countless requests from various individuals urgently appealing for action, for aid, for anything against the Indians reached his office; and he was quick to act.[46]

In Reid's first message to the Council, he declared firmly, if not wisely: "It is high time that sickly *sentimentality* should cease. 'Lo! the poor Indian,' is the exclamation of the fanatic and the pseudo-philanthropist. 'Lo, the poor *white* man!' is the ejaculation which all will utter, who have witnessed the inhuman butchery of women and children, and the massacres that have drenched the Territory in blood."[47] Throughout 1840 the war was one of his greatest concerns.[48] He devoted much energy to correspondence with Zachary Taylor, and when it became obvious that the general had little use for his suggestions, finally decided, "He is not the man for me."[49] He turned to an extensive correspondence with Secretary of War Joel R. Poinsett regarding strategy, finances, and the recruiting of troops. He also had to contend with accusations of political partisanship in his appointment of militia officers, some of them probably valid.[50] He quarreled with the local banks in an effort to secure funds to help finance the territorial militia.[51] He inadvertently aroused local confusion, northern humanitarian condemnation, and congressional ire when he purchased bloodhounds for use against the Indians.[52] He urged Legislative Council approval of volunteer brigades to protect frontier settlements.[53] But his greatest problem had to do with

45. E. A. Hitchcock to Samuel Hitchcock, [October 22?], 1840 (typed copy, Library of Florida History).

46. Fouraker, "Robert Raymond Reid," pp. 55, 61.

47. *House Journal* (1840), pp. 9-10.

48. R. R. Reid to Z. Taylor, April 2, 1840; Reid to J. R. Poinsett, May 9, 1840; Reid to F. L. Dancy, May 14, 1840; and other letters in "Letterbook of R. R. Reid."     49. Miller, *Bench and Bar in Georgia*, II, 224.

50. St. Augustine *Florida Herald*, July 17, 1840.

51. R. R. Reid to J. Williams, May 5, 1840 in "Letterbook of R. R. Reid."

52. *House Journal* (1840), p. 170; *Congressional Globe*, 26th Congress, 1st Session, VIII, 183.

53. *House Journal* (1840), pp. 168-71, 174; *Senate Journal* (1840), pp. 104-05.

33

the Florida volunteers—who would pay them and how much, and better still, how, when, and where could they be inducted into the United States Army.[54]

The Seminole War was hardly a partisan affair, though its operation occasionally became one. A good deal more debate was stimulated, however, regarding the volunteer militia. By April, 1838, after nearly two and a half years of war and with no end in sight, East Florida settlers were not only berating the regular army for its inability to capture a small band of marauding Seminoles, but also demanding to know why no local volunteers were being mustered into service.[55] Inaction continued on the militia question until Reid assumed office. Finally, in 1840, with the Council's blessing, the governor recruited 1,500 men for service. There was still the vital matter of paying the militia, and territorial finances were obviously inadequate. As a consequence, he urged upon the Secretary of War the propriety of transferring these troops into federal service. Poinsett acceded to the request, as well as to the suggestion that the regulars move south against the Indians, while the new recruits under General Leigh Read, Middle Florida Democrat, protected the settlements.[56]

The new strategy, and particularly the disposition and leadership of the militiamen, had great appeal in the territory. Floridians at last felt they were making a contribution, and at the same time, broken into small units, they were protecting their own homes, they would be near their families, and they might even be able to work their farms occasionally. Under this arrangement some progress was made during the rest of 1840 and early 1841. How successful this plan would have been had it been allowed to continue will never be known. With the advent of the new Whig administration in March, 1841, the existing program was scrapped. To begin with, Congress simply could not understand why it should pay men for protecting their own homes, and thus, no funds were appropriated. Then, John Bell, the new Secretary of War, ordered General Armistead, who had replaced Zachary Taylor in May, 1840, to muster the Florida volunteers out of federal service. This action, coupled with the government's refusal to pay the soldiers, precipitated a series of strong protests in the territory. "Is it just, is it equitable,"

54. R. R. Reid to J. R. Poinsett, July 29, August 3, 1840 in "Letterbook of R. R. Reid."

55. St. Augustine *Florida Herald*, April 28, 1838.

56. *Ibid.*, April 9, 1841.

a Democratic leader demanded, "that the master, for no fault, shall discharge the laborer, or the Government discharge the soldier, without pay for past services, without means of procuring a subsistence until other employment offers?"[57]

The militiamen, many of them frontier farmers and strongly Democratic, blamed their Whig delegate, Charles Downing, for not clarifying the situation in Congress or making the proper representations to the Harrison administration. They expressed themselves more positively in the May election for territorial delegate. Though there were other issues, the militia fiasco was a significant factor in David Levy's victory over Ward and Downing, particularly the latter in the areas under Indian attack. In frontier East Florida, Levy captured six counties, while Downing gained only one or possibly two counties. In Middle Florida Levy won four, Downing none.[58] By October, in apparently sharp contrast to his predecessor, he was successful in getting the administration to delay the removal of regular troops from still dangerous areas.[59] Again, though impossible to isolate from other issues of the day, the entire affair undoubtedly contributed in some measure to the third successive Democratic sweep of the Legislative Council elections that fall.

If the existence of the "banking monsters" and the problems connected with the Seminole War provided the Democrats with live ammunition in their battle for political ascendancy, the statehood and division issues proved to be less satisfactory additions to their arsenal. Indeed, it is extremely difficult to separate along political lines the advocates and opponents of statehood. From its inception as a significant movement in the mid-1830's, the drive for statehood cut across factional differences. Territorial sectionalism rather than parties proved to be the key to the situation.[60] On this issue even the press was influenced chiefly by region.[61] There was also the complicating demand for division which came from two areas of the territory. East Florida generally favored the creation of a new territory embodying peninsular Florida east of the Suwannee River.[62] In addition, some West Floridians favored the cession of a portion

57. *Ibid.*, April 2, 1841; Tallahassee *Floridian*, April 10, 1841.

58. See Table 3.

59. D. Levy to J. Tyler, October 6, 1841; J. C. Spencer to D. Levy, October 21, 1841 (Yulee Papers).     60. Thompson, "David L. Yulee," p. 26.

61. For example, in St. Augustine the Whig *News* and Democratic *Florida Herald* joined hands against statehood.

62. St. Augustine *News*, August 17, 1839; St. Augustine *Florida Herald*, April 2, 9, 1844.

of the western panhandle to Alabama, partially because many of them had spilled over from that older area. Even some East Floridians supported this idea on the grounds that it might eliminate Pensacola and possibly restore the earlier political and commercial importance of St. Augustine.[63]

In general, the statehood-division issues split the territory along the following lines: East Florida, largely against statehood and for division; Middle Florida, largely for statehood and against division; West Florida, divided on statehood, against division, and partly for cession.[64]

In East Florida large segments of the rank and file of both parties repeatedly expressed themselves against statehood and for division at public meetings in St. Augustine, Jacksonville, Mandarin, and other communities. By and large, they were led by many of the Whigs and some of the lesser Democrats.[65] They believed that the protracted Seminole War and the consequent economic dislocation called for continued federal assistance afforded by territorial status. Moreover, they feared that the obligations of statehood would inevitably lead to a rise in taxes. There were other considerations, too, including the fact that St. Augustine would probably be the capital of an East Florida territory. Distance was also another factor. With totally inadequate transportation, the eight-hundred-mile expanse between Key West and Pensacola appeared far too great for inclusion in a single state.[66]

In Middle Florida the great majority favored statehood. The Conservatives, many of whom were soon to be Whigs, supported admission to the Union during the late thirties because it would facilitate selling the Union Bank bonds abroad.[67] Even the Democrats, forcefully led by James D. Westcott, Jr., favored the statehood move.

63. Donald O. Hastings, "East-West Controversy and County Development in Territorial Florida" (Master's thesis, University of Florida, 1951), p. 169; J. B. Mool, "Florida in Federal Politics" (Master's thesis, Duke University, 1940), p. 7.

64. Mool, p. 7; Tallahassee *Floridian,* April 4, 1840; J. Beard to J. C. Calhoun, December 20, 1844, in *Annual Report of the American Historical Association for 1929* (Washington, 1930), p. 272; Thompson "David L. Yulee," pp. 26-27.

65. St. Augustine *News,* January 5, August 17, 1839; St. Augustine *Florida Herald,* April 2, 9, 1844.

66. St. Augustine *Florida Herald,* April 2, 9, 1844; Pensacola *Gazette,* March 19, 1834; St. Augustine *News,* February 15, 1845.

67. Reginald C. McGrane, *Foreign Bondholders and American State Debts* (New York, 1935), p. 233.

Any division, they felt, would ruin the territory and diminish the importance of their area.[68]

Despite the mass support of populous Middle Florida, the real leaders for admission to the Union came from the East Florida Democratic leaders. The statehood drive led in the first instance to the calling of the St. Joseph convention, and they had used it as a springboard for their own drive against the banks. Then, having created a thoroughly antibank constitution, they accepted the trend because statehood appeared to be a basic facet of popular government.[69] Governor Reid ridiculed apprehensions of a statehood tax burden. The *territorial* banks, he argued, had already placed a large burden upon the taxpayer![70] Moreover, he was joined by David Levy and other Democrats in a firm desire to bolster the strength and influence of their party with the national administration in Washington. Statehood meant electoral votes to contribute to the Democratic cause, and it held the promise of greater patronage. There would also be two senators and one representative to fight their battles, as well as the chance for achievement of high aspirations for some. Perhaps above all, there was the unvoiced recognition that statehood symbolized the triumph of their party principles, so important in an age when most of society sought the fulfillment of political equality.

It would appear somewhat paradoxical, then, that despite their pretensions of being truly representative of the people, the East Florida Democratic leaders were actually forwarding a movement contrary to the wishes of their own electorate. East Florida Whigs were aware of this inconsistency and sought to exploit it. During the Council elections in 1840, for example, they referred to their own candidates as "The *True Division* ticket," though with little effect.[71] In the following year's race for delegate, Levy focused his attack on the bank, conveniently permitting Ward and Downing to fight out the statehood-division issue. Moreover, early in 1839 a committee of the constitutional convention, composed of East Florida's Reid and Levy, along with Westcott, Thomas Baltzell, and Walker Anderson,

68. J. D. Westcott, Jr., to J. R. Poinsett, April 3, 1840 (Historical Society of Pennsylvania).

69. R. R. Reid to J. R. Poinsett, January 31, 1840 (Historical Society of Pennsylvania).

70. Reid, "Diary," May 6, 1840, quoted in Miller, *Bench and Bar in Georgia*, II, 225.

71. St. Augustine *News*, September 18, 1840. Italics added.

had already petitioned Congress for the admission of Florida to the Union.[72]

Nothing had come of these early moves. But once in Tallahassee, Governor Reid tactfully ignored the views of his own region, and in 1840 and 1841 his messages to the Council called for the adoption of statehood resolutions. Select committees of both houses supported his call in 1840, but subsequent votes revealed that only the lower body backed the move.[73] The 1841 session followed the same pattern. What had happened? Many of the East Florida divisionists, particularly the Senate Conservatives elected in 1838, joined forces with a group of Middle and West Florida bank supporters who opposed the antibank constitution, and their opposition blocked the resolution. In 1840 the East Florida Democrats swept the senatorial election, but the increasing antibank trend cemented the senators of the other two regions closer together. Strange it was, therefore, that Middle Florida bankmen, so ardently pro-statehood during the 1830's, should now oppose Council resolutions in its favor.

It was not until 1842 that the Democratic leaders, having effectively destroyed the banks, mobilized sufficient strength to secure the adoption of a statehood resolution.[74] From this point on David Levy, as Democratic delegate, spearheaded the drive for admission, emerging as "one of the most important influences in securing a majority opinion for statehood."[75] Levy's approach to the question, his grasp of cross-currents in Florida and Washington, and his handling of the entire issue reveal the firm hand of an astute and skilled political craftsman. He seemed never to have been inactive for a moment. With other leaders of his party he carefully cultivated the movement at home; when he thought it sufficiently strong there, he turned to the national scene. For three years Levy never waived an opportunity to raise the question in Congress, often to the despair of his surfeited colleagues. Then, in a conclusive effort to win additional adherents in Florida, he issued a 24-page *Circular Letter . . . to the People of Florida Relative to the Admission of Florida into the Union.*[76] There would be definite advantages, he wrote: One-half million acres for internal improvements; new

72. Dodd, *Florida Becomes a State*, pp. 329-33.
73. *Senate Journal* (1840), pp. 3, 35-40, 42-45, 84-85; *House Journal* (1840), pp. 69-71, 77-83, 114.
74. Dodd, pp. 382-83.
75. Edwin Williams, "Florida in the Union" (Ph.D. dissertation, University of North Carolina, 1951), p. 24.
76. N.p., 1844; printed copy in Yulee Papers.

38

impetus to immigration; probable payment for volunteer military duty; aid to education through land sales; division and distribution of the huge Spanish land grants; and the high privilege of self-government.

The Democrats, therefore, worked carefully and persistently on the statehood issue, but not until the mid-forties were they able to capitalize on it as they had the bank issue. Rather, the influence of the leaders, party, and organization served to mobilize public support and gradually convert the voters of Florida to *their* point of view. Thus, the Democratic party could represent, but it could also lead, the people.

There were other issues, too, which affected the Democratic struggle for power after 1838. Taxation, a perennial American party topic, also had its day in territorial Florida. Aside from the implications of the statehood conflict, the aftermath of the Panic of 1837 made the matter of taxes an increasingly vexing problem. The banking collapse aggravated the situation, and the Democrats, condemning the tax act of 1839, found another weapon with which they could attack the entrenched Conservative aristocracy. In his 1840 message to the Council, Governor Reid asked that only "light taxes, just in sufficient amount to meet the actual exigencies of the Territorial Treasury should be imposed." He also suggested that those who could not pay because of "unfortunate circumstances" should be exempt.[77] Still, little was done and the Democrats continued to argue in the Council elections of 1840 and 1841 that control of taxation must belong to the people. The strength—or repetition—of their arguments, the extent of their successive fall victories, and the acuteness of the depression by 1841 combined to convince the legislature in 1842 that the collection of taxes should be suspended.[78] The Democrats, having gained the initiative, needed to expend little effort in persuading a number of the Whig representatives to support their position.

Another issue which gave temporary strength to the Democratic cause had to do with a mortgage stay law. By 1841 the Democrats, in defense of the yeoman and in pursuit of his vote, called for a stay law. They promptly fulfilled their pledge during the session of 1842 by prohibiting the sale of property if some small amount were paid every two months toward satisfying an existing judgment.[79]

77. *House Journal* (1840), p. 17.
78. *Acts and Resolutions of the Legislative Council* (1842), p. 22.
79. *Ibid.*

By and large, however, the small farmers had relatively less to mortgage than the large planters, especially those indebted to the banks, who soon became the main beneficiary of the statute. Thus, the law proved to be a double-edged sword and was abandoned by the Democrats. But the Whigs would not abandon it and, looking to their welfare as well as for any stray Democratic votes they could garner, campaigned strongly for a stay law during the fall of 1842.[80] In 1843 James D. Westcott, Jr., staunch Middle Florida opponent of the Nucleus, led the Democratic assault on a new bill, questioning the extent to which it would really aid the "poor debtor."[81] But a shift in political power helped a Whig-sponsored stay measure become law, though within a few months it was declared unconstitutional by the judges of two separate district courts.[82] This, in turn, provided a basis for the new Democratic position. Taking a leaf from the earlier Whig defense of the banks, they self-righteously contended that "Bankrupt Laws and Stay Laws impair the obligations of contracts."[83]

There were still other problems which provoked individuals and groups on the Florida frontier, but none provided a basis for party action as did those already surveyed. Echoes of the movement for prison reform reached the territory, but few were noticeably moved. Governor Reid was almost alone in urging some changes in the criminal law. He pointed to the fact that the punishment for the maiming and wounding of cattle was "little less severe than that of man slaughter." The "cause of humanity" would be advanced, he felt, by establishing decent prisons and abolishing "the barbarous punishments of whipping, branding and pillory." He decried the absence of a single "secure jail in any one of the Counties" of East Florida, with the other districts being "quite as destitute."[84] Reid was a voice literally crying in a wilderness and he went largely unheeded. The carrying of rifles, pistols, and bowie knives was too commonplace to effect any real change. Barroom fights, knifings, and shootings were almost endemic.[85] One traveler observed that

80. Tallahassee *Florida Sentinel*, June 13, 1843.
81. *House Journal* (1843), p. 11.
82. St. Augustine *Florida Herald*, June 26, 1843.
83. St. Augustine *News*, April 26, 1845. By this time, the *News* had become a Democratic paper.
84. *House Journal* (1840), p. 16.
85. Comte Francis de Castelnau, "Essay on Middle Florida, 1837-38," *Florida Historical Quarterly*, XXVI (January, 1948), 236-37; J. Benwell, *An Englishman's Travels in America* (London, n.d.), p. 150; St. Augustine

"those clinging to the strictest rule in matters of religion, good order, and morals, must for a while be considered as forming a minority."[86]

The temperance movement was another crusade of the era which managed to filter into the territory and win some adherents among small local groups. But the frontier norm was hardly one of abstinence. The few temperance meetings were grimly ignored, though on one occasion a Tallahassee session was broken up by a group of irate citizens who pledged themselves to drink, if not to drunkenness.[87] Bishop Whipple's survey of the Florida scene in 1843 left him aghast, and he announced that the East Florida frontier community of Black Creek came "the nearest to total depravity of any village I have ever seen. . . ."[88] In any event, alcoholic refreshment remained a prominent part of daily life. Besides, what would the Democratic barbecues, campaign gatherings, and victory celebrations, with their countless toasts, have been without spiritous inspiration?

*News*, January 5, 1839; Quincy *Sentinel*, February 19, 1841; Apalachicola *Commercial Advertiser*, November 4, 1843.

86. Charles J. Latrobe, *The Rambler in North America* (New York, 1835), II, 49-52.

87. *Ibid.*

88. *Bishop Whipple's Southern Diary*, p. 71.

41

# 4. AIDS TO SUCCESS

O ne of the most significant forces contributing to the political triumph of the Democratic party in Florida was the organization created by its leaders following the St. Joseph convention. The Democratic Republican meeting in that convention town on January 11, 1839, was the beginning of a remarkably successful organizational drive. Robert Raymond Reid, by virtue of his position in the territory, his national party connections, and his service as convention chairman, became in effect titular head of the party. But it was David Levy and James D. Westcott, Jr., who emerged as the real driving forces in their respective East and Middle Florida sections, and to a lesser degree Walker Anderson in West Florida. Moreover, when Reid died in the yellow fever epidemic of 1841, Levy, as his legal protégé and the newly elected delegate to Congress, became the territory's leading Democrat.

In the meantime, with the enthusiasm generated by the first party meeting at St. Joseph still high, the Democratic delegates returned to their respective counties to begin the task of creating local organizations at the proverbial grass-roots level. Their efforts brought prompt results. By the summer and early fall of 1839 county Democratic meetings were being staged in most parts of the territory. The Alachua County Democratic Republican Anti-Bankites, for example, met at Newnansville on August 22, there to nominate Jesse Carter for the lower house of the Council.[1] Similar meetings were held in most parts of frontier East Florida—in St. Johns, Duval, Nassau, and Columbia counties.[2] In more populous Middle Florida, particularly in Leon County, precinct groups were the first step. On July 27, 1839, James A. Berthelot chaired a Tallahassee precinct meeting at the Planter's Hotel. Its object? To unite with other precincts of the county in nominating suitable candidates for the coming legislative elections.[3] They continued their activities, invariably affording different local supporters an opportunity to serve as chairman and secretary of their sessions.[4] In addition, resolutions committees made their contribution, and delegates were selected for a county conven-

1. St. Augustine *Florida Herald,* September 15, 1839.
2. *Ibid.,* July 24, 1840.
3. *Ibid.,* August 22, 1839.
4. Tallahassee *Floridian,* August 1, 1840.

tion. Other Middle and West Florida county groups were also formed during 1839 and 1840.[5]

Within a year enough county Democratic organizations were operating to merit regional gatherings. Besides, the creation of an upper house for the Council in 1838 meant that a group of senators were to be elected on a district rather than on a county basis. This provided the Democrats not only with a rationale for convening intercounty meetings, but also a means whereby they could consolidate their organization. In August of 1840 county delegates convened at Black Creek for an East Florida conclave, and three Democratic candidates were nominated "to represent the people" in the territorial Senate.[6] Two weeks later, on August 22, all five counties of Middle Florida sent delegates to Monticello for a similar convention.[7] These regional affairs were successful in bringing the county leaders together, though full attendance was not always possible because of "sickness," "Indian depredations," and "the insalubrity of the weather."[8]

There remained only the need for creating some territorial-wide organization to cap the party's pyramidal structure. This came with the holding of informal party caucuses during the annual meetings of the Legislative Council. One of the earliest of such meetings occurred on March 3, 1840, when the Democratic members of the Council, together with prominent leaders from various sections of the territory, gathered in the chamber of the lower house. They gave careful attention to the matter of geography. Leigh Read (Leon County) was named chairman. Elias E. Blackburn (Jefferson), Jesse Carter (Alachua), and Joseph Irwin (Jackson) won vice-presidencies; Edmund Bird (Alachua) and Samuel S. Sibley (Leon) served as secretaries; and Nathaniel W. Walker, Hugh Archer, James A. Berthelot, John L. Taylor, Daniel Bell, Walker Anderson, I. G. Searcy, Westcott, and Levy comprised a resolutions committee. In addition to discussing local problems and legislative positions, they announced their support of Van Buren over Harrison for the Presidency.[9]

Between legislative caucuses and county or regional conventions,

5. Quincy *Sentinel*, August 21, 1840.
6. St. Augustine *Florida Herald*, July 24, 1840; D. Levy to J. L. Doggett *et al.*, September 7, 1840 (copy, Yulee Papers).
7. Quincy *Sentinel*, August 21, 1840.
8. Tallahassee *Floridian*, August 29, 1840.
9. St. Augustine *Florida Herald*, April 2, 1840.

committees of correspondence spurred local interest and maintained contact with other groups.[10] To enlarge the area of popular participation, these committees were invariably large. The General Committee of Correspondence of the Democratic (Loco-Foco) Party of Leon County, for example, contained ten members at its meeting on March 21, 1840.[11]

Another device to strengthen the organization was the "barbecue." These popular local assemblages also served to spread the party program and win new adherents. Ample food and drink made them festive as well as political affairs. Reasons to stage these barbecues were relatively easy to find. The St. Johns Democrats, for example, met in St. Augustine at Colonel Gue's Long Room on March 16, 1839, to celebrate the stand of their convention and Council delegates "against the encroachments of monied aristocracies and soulless corporations."[12] Other instances celebrated the glories of a local or territorial politician, occasioning "a feasting and drinking bout" of sizeable proportions.[13]

These parties, carefully planned for political effect, invoked the services of a large number of local citizens. For example, when news reached St. Augustine in the early fall of 1844 that David Levy would pass through the city on his way back to Washington, the political wheels began to turn. A committee was organized to meet him at the city gates; a committee of thirteen was appointed to arrange the barbecue; a committee of ten was selected to invite the delegate; and still another committee took charge of general arrangements. An invitation was sent, and Levy's letter of acceptance included a lengthy glorification of the Democratic party as well as a review of his own accomplishments in Congress. When the Democratic barbecue finally took place on November 28, it was a gala affair. Toasts were offered to the newly elected Polk, to Levy, and down through the entire chain of Democratic command, to people's government, to democracy and the Democracy, to the end of the Indians, to each other and all present, and they were terminated only by nightfall. This gathering, typical of its kind throughout Florida at the time, certainly illustrated the principle of maximum popular participation.[14]

10. *Ibid.*, August 22, 1839; Tallahassee *Floridian*, March 21, 1840.
11. Tallahassee *Floridian*, March 21, 1840.
12. St. Augustine *Florida Herald*, March 21, 1839.
13. St. Augustine *News*, October 29, 1842.
14. St. Augustine *Florida Herald*, November 26, December 3, 1844.

The key to the rapid rise of the Democrats during the early 1840's, then, was their organization, particularly as it operated through the various conventions. These local, county, and district meetings usually followed the same pattern. All interested citizens were invited to attend the local or precinct meetings. When a sufficient number had gathered, a Democrat of some local prominence was called to the chair and another appointed secretary. Then a more prominent leader from that or some other community explained the object of the meeting. Following this main speech of the evening, a committee was appointed by the chairman—with or without general approval—to nominate delegates to the county convention. The committee withdrew, made its selections—or received appropriate suggestions—and returned to present the slate to the meeting. When a general vote of approval of the candidates had been secured, a large local committee of correspondence was appointed to keep in touch with other precincts and, above all, to help get out the vote.

At the county level the procedure was pretty much the same. Those called on to serve as chairman and secretary and to present the main speech were, of course, proportionately more prominent Democrats. Again a committee presented nominations to the floor. This time the convention delegates selected those who would serve as the party's nominee, or nominees, in the county race for the lower house of the Council. When district conventions were to be held to nominate candidates for the Senate of the Council, another committee of the county convention offered a slate from which those assembled elected delegates to the regional meetings.[15] In practice the procedures were not quite so formidable, nor were the successive echelons too far removed from the original participants. In most instances county delegates were also district delegates and, on occasions, the precinct sessions sent representatives directly to the district meetings to supplement the delegates elected at the county conventions.

The reasonably democratic machinery of the Democratic party was, therefore, instrumental in its rise. Significant also was the widespread appeal of its campaign tactics. For some the new methods were appalling, even shocking, but for the Democrats it meant votes, and their successes dictated continued use of these techniques. Special publications were utilized in hotly contested campaigns. In the 1841 election for delegate, when Levy opposed both Ward and

15. St. Augustine *News,* April 19, 1845.

45

Downing, the Democrats were printing two special papers. In East Florida *The Anti-Bankite* was available from March 1 to the May election for twenty-five cents. In Middle Florida, where the anti-bank sentiment was not as violent, a paper called *The People's Friend* emanated from Tallahassee and was also devoted entirely to Levy's campaign.[16]

Campaign songs, slogans, and verses were bestowed upon an unsuspecting electorate. The music of the "St. Augustine Loco Foco Dance," provided with lyrics, made a stirring ballad of the times!

> *Huzza! for the loco focos!*
> *Their banner floats on high,*
> *It flutters in the sea-breeze,*
> *And glitters in the sky.*
> *We'd follow where it leads us,*
> *Regardless who oppose,*
> *Success to the Loco Focos,*
> *Confusion to their foes![17]*

One wonders how many votes these doggerels gained for the Democrats.

Throughout the territory, and particularly in East Florida, the older, Spanish-speaking residents were not lost to the Democratic cause. Men like Buckingham Smith and John M. Fontane, St. Johns County Democratic candidates for the Council in 1840, placed Spanish as well as English political advertisements in the local press.[18]

The really significant campaign technique was, of course, the political speech. Democratic candidates took to the stump all over Florida. The size of their audiences varied, depending upon the political complexion of the newspaper making the report. The Democratic newspapers saw tremendous crowds of enthusiastic supporters; the opposition noted a few friends, some of the opposition, and many persons not entitled to vote. The speeches themselves also varied. Some were full of egotistical nonsense, vulgarity was common, and exaggeration was much in evidence. Some despaired that the particular contest was merely one of words. Excessive partisan zeal, personal slurs, and rousing emotional and tearful appeals were

16. Thompson, "David L. Yulee," p. 23; St. Augustine *Florida Herald,* April 16, 1841.
17. St. Augustine *Florida Herald,* October 17, 1840.
18. *Ibid.,* October 10, 1840.

prominently displayed or utilized. Extreme language of the variety used today only in some private conversation was placed before the public through speech and press. Levy's analysis of Charles Downing in 1840 was not untypical: "I hold him to be a truckler in politics, treacherous and unfaithful alike in his public and private relations, a secret slanderer and a public libeller, and possessed of scarcely honesty enough to elevate him above the common swindler."[19]

Combined with the oratorical color and bombast were issues minutely and often embarrassingly exposed to public scrutiny. In the actual voting process the Democrats adopted a method which they hoped would help their cause, particularly among those of limited literacy. Democratic papers, just prior to the canvass, would devote a column to printing the candidate's name in each of a series of boxes which could serve as actual ballots. Below was the statement, "The friends of [the candidate] can cut them off on the day of election and use them."[20] It is assumed that no voter exceeded his quota.

Election victories also brought innovations to Florida. The immediate reaction to a Democratic triumph was a party celebration of sizeable magnitude. A Whig newspaper glumly and succinctly summarized one such orgy with the report that "there was considerable rejoicing, lots of liquor drunk, and sundry broken heads!"[21] Shortly thereafter, when sobriety had returned, the new official extended his thanks to the electorate through the press and expressed a wish to serve all the people.[22]

Especially significant in the growth of the Florida Democratic party were the newspapers. Indeed, the Democratic press was an intimate part of the party, and their respective fortunes were intimately related. There was no prouder nor more profitable announcement, for example, than the newspaper item which read "The Senate, on Wednesday last elected the conductor of this paper printer to that honorable body." Equally cheering was news of a Governor Reid letter that all orders, laws, and resolutions of the late Legislative Council were to be published in the Pensacola

19. Quincy *Sentinel*, September 4, 1840; *Bishop Whipple's Southern Diary*, p. 38; St. Augustine *Florida Herald*, December 4, 1840, April 30, 1841; Tallahassee *Florida Sentinel*, March 5, 1844.

20. St. Augustine *Florida Herald*, April 17, 1843.

21. St. Augustine *News*, October 17, 1840.

22. Tallahassee *Floridian*, June 26, 1841; St. Augustine *Florida Herald*, June 11, 1841.

*Gazette,* the Tallahassee *Floridian,* and the St. Augustine *Florida Herald and Southern Democrat.*[23]

Despite this inducement, there were some territorial papers that attempted a nonpartisan course. In 1839 Joseph Crosbey of the Apalachicola *Courier* hoped, "by shunning the dangerous extremes of party feeling . . . to establish a Free and Independent Press."[24] He was not particularly successful. Neither was the St. Joseph *Times* the following year when it opened its columns to all parties, only to face the condemnation of its Whig friends.[25] Perhaps the major exception was the Pensacola *Gazette,* which pursued a kind of benevolent neutrality toward the Whigs. Much of its success undoubtedly derived from the fact that it was the only paper at the time in that thriving West Florida port.

In Middle Florida the Tallahassee *Floridian* was the key Democratic organ and center of controversy. Its patron saint was James D. Westcott, Jr. It fought the St. Joseph *Times,* the Quincy *Sentinel,* and all other comers. When Joseph Clisby, *Sentinel* editor, moved his press to Tallahassee, the Tallahassee *Florida Sentinel* became the *Floridian's* major rival. The gentlemen who ran these papers were not averse to expressing candid opinions of each other or of their respective journalistic efforts. Party strife frequently prompted comments such as "filthy sheet" and "editorially prostituted," and brought retorts such as "We look beyond the imbecile and irresponsible monarch on the throne [the editor] to the cunning and craft minister of his crimes and passions [local Democratic leader, in this instance, Westcott]."[26]

The East Florida counterpart of the Tallahassee battle between the *Floridian* and *Sentinel* took place in St. Augustine between the *Florida Herald* and the *News.* The *Florida Herald's* ardent support of Reid, Levy, and other Democrats led the *News* to print a number of lively remarks, including the statement that the *Herald's* editor, James M. Gould, was "a liar" and his paper a "dirty vehicle of abuse, malignancy and evil speaking."[27] The response was generally even less flattering.

Late in 1842 the Tallahassee *Florida Sentinel* suggested that the *Herald* and *News* bury the hatchet and come to the capital the

23. March 16, 1841, "R. R. Reid Letterbook, December 1839—April 1841" (Microfilm Records of the States, Florida, E. 2).

24. St. Joseph *Times,* October 8, 1839.     25. *Ibid,* August 14, 1840.

26. *Ibid.,* May 5, 1840; Quincy *Sentinel,* December 11, 1840.

27. July 6, 1839, August 21, 1840.

following January for a temperance convention. The *News* replied editorially, "For our part we rather imagine the journey too long a one, merely to see folks drink cold water! What say you, neighbor Gould?"[28] On such rare occasions the two newspapers saw eye to eye. In the main, however, the Democratic press hardly allowed itself to agree with the Whigs. Their slogans reflected the issues of the day: "Principles and the People" (St. Augustine *Florida Herald*); "Laissez nous Faire" (Tallahassee *Floridian*); and "Separation from Banks" (Tallahassee *Southern Journal*).[29] Their editorials, their political advertisements, their delineation of the issues, and their special headings at election time in support of particular candidates made them a vital, even indispensable, part of the Democratic movement. Their biting rhymes, their sarcasm, their extensive coverage of Democratic speeches, announcements, platforms, meetings, and conventions, their running condemnation of the opposition, their line-by-line refutation of Whig statements, and an almost fanatical defense of their cause generated popular excitement and stirred the electorate. The Democratic press was clearly part and parcel of the Democratic rise to power.

Equally vital to the Democratic ascendancy were the national contacts of some of the party leaders, and the patronage which ensued. Once the Democrats initiated their organizational drive in 1839, territorial leaders hastened to strengthen ties with party and administration leaders in Washington. Especially fruitful would be Robert Reid's friendship with John Forsyth and Joel R. Poinsett, Secretaries of State and War.[30] Through them he gained more ready access to Van Buren. In 1840 five prominent Florida Democrats notified the President that David Levy had been designated as their representative "to visit Washington and make your Excellency acquainted with the true state of affairs here."[31] The following month, in an effort to bolster Levy's hand in the capital, Reid advised Poinsett that "the march of Principle is so slow—the movement of faction so alert—that unless our Democracy is *Sustained* at Washington, its movements must be retrograde."[32]

Thanks to such early forays into the national arena, Levy was

28. November 26, 1842.      29. Thompson, "David L. Yulee," p. 16.

30. A considerable Reid-Poinsett correspondence is located among the latter's papers at the Historical Society of Pennsylvania.

31. R. R. Reid, J. McCants, I. G. Searcy, John Branch, and L. Read to M. Van Buren, March 5, 1840 (Van Buren Papers, Library of Congress).

32. R. R. Reid to J. R. Poinsett, April 15, 1840 (Historical Society of Pennsylvania).

soon able to make his own way. Charles Wickliffe, soon to be his father-in-law and already John Tyler's Postmaster General, was a splendid contact. As delegate, Levy managed to secure almost immediately a congressional appropriation to pay the Florida volunteer militia. This news, if not the money, reached the territory in time to have a favorable influence on the 1841 fall elections.[33] There were other party ties that ran between Washington and Florida, but none were so binding as those which bore tangible results: jobs!

In 1839 Levy boldly addressed a long memorandum to President Van Buren on the state of the Florida Democratic party. After an analysis of the obstacles it faced, including the need for more and capable leaders, he proposed:

That to form a nucleus to the Democratic Party, afford leaders and infuse vigor into its organization, *all the offices in Florida, from highest to lowest,* should be immediately filled with active thorough-going democrats mostly from the states. I should even say *all* from abroad, but some of the offices would be too small to induce persons to remove to Florida and some few selections of influential Floridians will be necessary to keep the people in humor.

In making the selections from abroad persons should be taken from such of the different states as have furnished most of the emigrants, that they may gather around them their respective clans.[34]

The *Florida Herald* echoed the private communiqué in its demand that every officer living on the people's money should support the people's cause.[35] Despite problems of its own, the national administration responded reasonably fast, though not all of Van Buren's appointments pleased the territorial Democrats.[36]

The major administration move was the removal of Richard K. Call and the appointment of Robert R. Reid as governor of the territory. As early as 1835, when Reid had been district judge for three years, he expressed the hope that "Forsyth might do something for me." When there was some talk of Forsyth leaving the Cabinet, Reid wrote in his diary, "Hope not, both for his sake and

33. St. Augustine *Florida Herald,* September 17,1841.
34. D. Levy, "Brief remarks concerning the Democratic cause in Florida, with a suggestion, respectfully submitted to the President" (Van Buren Papers).
35. September 5, 1839.
36. R. R. Reid to J. R. Poinsett, April 15, 1840 (Historical Society of Pennsylvania).

mine."[37] But by late 1839 Forsyth and Poinsett had found the proper occasion for Reid's advancement.[38] Along with Reid, of course, came Joseph McCants as secretary of the territory.

In addition to giving the Democrats control over the territorial administration, national patronage was also used to bolster the party's strength in certain areas, as well as to reward the faithful. In 1840, for example, Pensacola's Walker Anderson asked Poinsett to back Democratic friends in Escambia County, where the party was rather weak.[39] From Tallahassee Reid urged that Samuel S. Sibley, editor of the *Floridian*, be appointed local postmaster, with the admonition "should he not be appointed—it will have a decidedly bad effect."[40] From St. Augustine Levy persuaded Charles Wickliffe to replace the existing postmaster with John M. Fontane, a faithful Democrat who had served in the Legislative Council in 1841.[41]

After Reid's death, Levy spearheaded the job hunt. Thanks to Wickliffe, it was not entirely fruitless, for President Tyler proved to be something of a disappointment. Levy reported to Westcott in 1842 "that Mr Tyler is a weak man. . . . The members and senators of both parties tell me on all sides that they hardly ever know anything of appts in their Districts till the name goes in."[42] James K. Polk was a substantial improvement, for Levy was not only able to get his quota of appointments, but also managed to time them to suit the party's convenience. For example, he notified Westcott in 1845, "You may . . . say that no appointments will be made by the President of the U.S. in Florida until after the state is organized."[43] Two weeks later, when a key position at the Pensacola Navy Agency became available, he urged Polk to keep it open "in the same manner as the other offices in Florida, until the elections are over here."[44]

The Democratic cause in the early forties was also fostered by another aspect of the patronage system. Aside from key Washington

37. Quoted in Fouraker, "Robert Raymond Reid," pp. 7, 9.

38. D. Levy to J. R. Poinsett, January 19, 1839 [?] (Historical Society of Pennsylvania). Though dated 1839, the letter was undoubtedly written in 1840.

39. W. Anderson to J. R. Poinsett, August 27, 1840 (Historical Society of Pennsylvania).

40. R. R. Reid to J. R. Poinsett, April 15, 1840 (Historical Society of Pennsylvania).    41. St. Augustine *Florida Herald*, September 25, 1843.

42. D. Levy to J. D. Westcott, Jr., May 6, 1842 (copy, Yulee Papers).

43. D. Levy to J. D. Westcott, Jr., March 21, 1845 (copy, Yulee Papers).

44. D. Levy to J. K. Polk, April 5, 1845 (Polk Papers, Library of Congress).

appointments, the flow of new positions from Tallahassee assumed considerable proportions. When Reid left St. Augustine to take up his duties as governor, Democratic aspirants for local jobs received new hope. Actually, the Whigs were not entirely ignored, receiving county judgeships in Gadsden, Calhoun, and Leon, territorial auditor, and some militia commands. But the opposition criticism of Reid as a "party man" who showed a strong desire "to promote and sustain his party by every means in his power" was somewhat justified.[45]

Beginning the moment he assumed the office in January, 1840, Reid swept the old order out, and the wholesale appointment of Democrats followed. There were military positions: quartermaster general, adjutant general, militia commanders; and there were nonmilitary positions: county judges, auctioneers, justices of the peace, tax collectors, court clerks, and notaries public—to say nothing of his influence in the selection of marshals, district attorneys, district judges, and postmasters. During his early months in office, literally dozens of offices were filled—an aide-de-camp, an auctioneer for the town of Port Leon, a Calhoun County tax collector, a notary public for the town of St. Marks, an Alachua County judge, Escambia County justices of the peace, ad infinitum.[46] The list was immense and it continued to grow, aided, of course, by the creation of new communities and counties. By 1842 the number of county court judges, auctioneers, justices of the peace, and notaries public *alone* reached 418. A county breakdown reveals the following distribution:[47]

| Alachua | 22 | Gadsden | 23 | Mosquito | 4 |
|---|---|---|---|---|---|
| Columbia | 17 | Hamilton | 14 | Monroe | 23 |
| Calhoun | 16 | Hillsborough | 6 | Nassau | 12 |
| Duval | 43 | Jackson | 29 | St. Johns | 27 |
| Dade | 10 | Jefferson | 16 | Walton | 10 |
| Escambia | 35 | Leon | 66 | Washington | 8 |
| Franklin | 28 | Madison | 9 | | |

It might be observed that in 1843 the vote for territorial delegate was 4,544, making the *total* number of political appointees in Florida almost 10 per cent of the electorate. The percentage is even more spectacular if one remembers that the overwhelming majority

45. St. Augustine *News*, January 3, 1840; St. Augustine *Florida Herald*, October 3, 1840.
46. "R. R. Reid Letterbook."     47. *House Journal* (1842), Appendix.

of those government officeholders were Democrats and that the Democratic party received 2,807 votes.

The Democratic triumphs during the 1840's were also aided by the general tide of immigration which flowed into this southern territory. From New Jersey and upstate New York small groups moved to various sections of South Florida. Most of the migrants, however, came from the South, particularly from South Carolina, Georgia, and Alabama.[48] They settled all over the territory, but most of them took up lands in the frontier portions of East Florida. There was still ample room for even more newcomers, if only the Seminole question could finally be settled.

A partial solution to this problem originated in the Headquarters of the Army of Florida in 1841, when Colonel W. J. Worth urged that armed settlers be encouraged to come into the more southern areas of East Florida.[49] This, he suggested, would have "a powerful influence upon the savage." David Levy picked up the idea and, working through a number of sympathetic congressmen, especially Senator Thomas Hart Benton, secured the passage of the Florida Armed Occupation Act on August 4, 1842.[50] The law was operative for a year, until December 1, 1843, during which time an armed settler properly registered at the nearest Land Office received a free grant of 160 acres.[51]

The response was favorable. During 1843, 1,184 permits were issued to 615 heads of families and 569 single men (many of whose families came later), totaling 189,440 acres.[52] More than half came from the Carolinas, Georgia, and Alabama, moving overland or by steamers from Charleston and Savannah. Most of the rest came from older settled areas within the territory itself. The experience of one, Jeremiah Dodson, was undoubtedly typical of the yeoman influx. In a letter to the register of the Land Office at Newnansville, Alachua County, where almost three-quarters of the permits were issued, he wrote: "I have come here from N. Carolina, with two good guns and several hundred rounds of ammunition; have

48. Thompson, "David L. Yulee," p. 11; *Bishop Whipple's Southern Diary*, p. 27.

49. Colonel W. J. Worth to Major D. Wilcox, June 24, 1841, in St. Augustine *Florida Herald*, July 9, 1841.

50. St. Augustine *Florida Herald*, July 17, 1843.

51. Dodd, "Letters from East Florida," *Florida Historical Quarterly*, XV (July, 1936), p. 51.

52. "Actual Settlements in Florida, under the Armed Occupation Law," 28th Congress, 1st Session, *House of Representatives Document No. 70*, p. 56.

pitched my tent and gone to work as an armed occupant should do, in order to add value to the soil and make it worth defending, if a savage foe should assault. I therefore wish you to be so kind as to issue my permit and send it by the bearer hereof."[53]

In the meantime, by 1843, the Indian struggle had reached an end "when little more than a hundred warriors remained." Most of the remaining Seminoles had been killed or had acquiesced in the move to the west.[54] William Cullen Bryant, observing the new frontier in April, 1843, reported somewhat over-enthusiastically to his readers, "Now that the Indian war is ended, colonization has revived and people are thronging into the country to take advantage of the law which assigns a hundred and sixty acres to every actual settler."[55]

The immigrant influx into Florida during this period was, therefore, substantial, though by no means overwhelming. It is difficult, if not impossible, to ascertain individual voting records. But it is clear that in territorial-wide elections between 1839 and 1845 the Democrats increasingly gained the upper hand. In analyzing those elections—for delegate in 1839, 1841, 1843 and for congressional representative in 1845—the Democrats polled 7 per cent, 52 per cent, 76 per cent, and 68 per cent of the East Florida votes. Of the ballots cast in East *and* Middle Florida for the same posts and period, the Democrats captured 42 per cent, 48 per cent, 66 per cent, and 65 per cent of the votes respectively. The total East Florida vote in the territorial-wide election in 1839 was 1,415; by 1845 it was 2,259. Middle Florida jumped from 1,747 to 2,076, and West Florida increased only slightly from 1,413 to 1,528.[56] How much of this absolute increase merely represented a larger popular participation and how much was the result of immigration cannot be ascertained. But it is clear that both the absolute and relative increases were greater in East Florida. Moreover, since East Florida gained the largest number of newcomers, it may reasonably be assumed, acknowledging that statistical correlation does not definitively establish causation, that immigration contributed in some measure to the cause of the Florida Democrats.

Finally, in analyzing the varied factors which aided the ascendancy of the Democratic party after 1838, the matter of the general

53. St. Augustine *Florida Herald*, July 17, 1843.
54. Patrick, *Florida Under Five Flags*, p. 35.
55. *Letters of a Traveller, or, Notes of things seen in Europe and America* (New York, 1850), p. 122.    56. See Table 3.

philosophy which guided the movement must be raised. It can be stated quite simply that the democratic temper of the age constituted the Florida party's basic outlook. This is not meant to imply that all of its leaders or supporters were necessarily imbued with or committed to all the ideals and practices of democracy. It does mean that whatever individual political goals, economic motivations, and social aspirations were involved, most of the party's leaders and those who voted for them did at least accept the broad principles implicit in the democratic ideology of the period.

To the Florida Democrats of the late thirties and early forties the democratic ideology constituted a revolt against all monopolies, political, economic, or social. It challenged existing political power held by virtue of the opposition's "behind-the-scenes manipulation," caucus nominations, inadequate appeals to the electorate, and "government by clique."[57] It condemned economic privilege created by legislative grants of exclusive charters, as well as intimate connections between government and an economic elite.[58] And it opposed the social aristocracy which had emerged in earlier territorial days. The appeal, then, was for an order devoid of any kind of special privilege.

Toward that end the party's leaders affirmed their belief in a political arrangement which encouraged the maximum participation of all citizens. All phases of the political process were to be open to all, regardless of Spanish, French, or English origins. There was to be "no picking and choosing" of any kind. Nor was there to be any connection between church and state. In short, power was to reside *in* and be exercised *by* the people themselves.[59] They wholeheartedly embraced the economic principle of free enterprise, without at the same time accepting all of the theoretical implications of laissez faire. Adhering to the view of equal opportunity, they protested against "corporate privilege," as well as "great land" and "townmaking speculators." They vilified legislation for the benefit of selected individuals and quoted with approval the address made by George Bancroft on the Fourth of July, 1826, that "laws should favor the diffusion of property and its easy acquisition, not the concentration of it in the hands of a few to the impoverishment

57. Doherty, *The Whigs of Florida*, p. 1; Thompson, "David L. Yulee," pp. 11, 16.

58. Thompson, pp. 12, 16; St. Augustine *Florida Herald*, November 7, 1840.

59. St. Augustine *Florida Herald*, March 28, April 11, 1839, November 7, 1840.

of the many."[60] Equally repugnant was the existence of an aristocracy, for it called forth unwarranted societal distinctions. They held that all men were born equal and that no man should assume a special station in life based upon connections or ancestry. Were it not for the work of "the people," it was argued, "all the *gentlemen* in the world would in a mighty short time be laid where all 'distinctions' are ended."[61] The efforts of an individual, coupled with the benefits of education universally diffused, should be the proper means of achieving his status. This, then, was the basic ideology of the Democratic party and its practical task was to approximate it.[62]

Of course, there was a gap of varying proportions between the party's philosophy and its pronouncements on the one hand, and the party's practices and its actualities on the other. With the passage of time this gap was often obscured and the ideal fused into the real. Indeed, within two decades one writer appraising the Florida scene in 1840 wrote: "There was at that particular juncture, a severe contest raging between the aristocracy and the people— between the Money-Power and the Democracy—each contending for the mastery, each resolved to do or die."[63] Thus despite the disparity, the general philosophy which engrossed the Democratic party served as an important rallying point, and the movement was able to ride the tide of a bull market in democracy.

Moreover, in pursuit of its announced objectives, the Democratic leaders sought some guideposts, something which would give them a connection with the past and a sense of continuity. For these latter-day Florida Democrats of the "Age of Jackson," the hero of New Orleans, though a "venerable and exalted patriot," was not yet the great political symbol he would become later.[64] Rather, it was to Mr. Jefferson that these men turned. His critique of aristocracy, banking institutions, and "monied corporations" struck a responsive chord; his defense of the yeoman became part of their cause and his

60. D. Levy to J. L. Doggett and J. T. Broer, September 7, 1840, in Thompson, "David L. Yulee," pp. 246-48; D. Levy to M. Van Buren, n.d., 1839 (Van Buren Papers); St. Augustine *Florida Herald*, December 3, 1844; St. Augustine *News*, April 26, 1845.

61. St. Augustine *Florida Herald*, April 4, 1839.

62. St. Augustine *News*, April 26, 1845; St. Augustine *Florida Herald*, March 28, April 4, 1839, March 5, 1840, December 3, 1844; Pensacola *Gazette*, October 30, 1841.

63. Miller, *Bench and Bar in Georgia*, II, 236.

64. Tallahassee *Star of Florida*, June 27, 1845.

enemies became theirs.[65] Here then was the historical continuity which gave them inspiration. The certainty of their cause was based on still higher grounds. Clearly, the path of democracy was the true one, and after all, "When did Truth fail in the assertion of its supremacy? Its progress may be impeded by the barriers of Error, and, clouded by the smoke of the incense which the selfish are ever pouring upon the altars of Interest, its steps may be unheeded, but *there is a principle at work in Nature* which bears it onward to triumph, surely and irresistably [*sic*] as the march of Fate."[66] Thomas Jefferson and the laws of nature, then, provided the historical and philosophic assumptions upon which the leaders based their cause. In all the literature on the Florida Democratic movement between 1838 and 1845 Andrew Jackson is rarely, if ever, mentioned. His image was probably still too real to serve their purpose, and in territorial Florida his name was still too closely tied to the origins of the opposition.

65. St. Joseph *Times,* June 9, 1840; innumerable issues of the Tallahassee *Floridian* and the St. Augustine *Florida Herald,* particularly the latter's January, 1841, issues.

66. Speech of D. Levy, April 1, 1839, in St. Augustine *Florida Herald,* April 11, 1839. Italics added.

# 5. SOCIAL STRATIFICATION

The issues which were so vigorously debated in the course of the Democratic rise to power in Florida reflected in considerable measure the divergent views and aspirations of various elements in late territorial society. Unfortunately for those with a bent for quantification, neither the social stratification of that era nor a class basis of its political parties can be delineated with any great degree of precision. Retreat must be made, therefore, to reasonably valid generalization. To begin with, economic and social differences, though often substantial and all too real, cannot be neatly categorized. Not only were class lines blurred, but the relatively high degree of geographic and social mobility tended to soften the pressure of discontent between existing groups. Again, pre-existing attitudes, local problems, personalities, and particularly the area of origin all served to negate any clear-cut party division on a strictly economic basis. Moreover, in the creation of the Democratic party in Florida, a number of different social forces, some of them seemingly contradictory, found themselves aligned in a common political front.

In terms of sheer bulk, the small, independent agrarians were probably of primary importance to the Democratic cause.[1] The average yeoman, variously described as "kind," "generous," and "careless," enjoyed few of the available luxuries of his day.[2] His was a genuinely grueling, lonely, and often tedious existence. For some the burdens of frontier or rural life were eased by the ownership of one or two slaves. The largest percentage of these small slaveholders were concentrated in Middle Florida. The majority of the farmers however, particularly those located in the frontier area of East Florida, were not slaveholders.[3] Many of these small farmers tended to emulate the planters in the cultivation of cotton and tobacco, depending, of course, upon the nature of the soil in their area. In addition, they found the production of sugar cane and rice exceedingly profitable, while corn, potatoes, and some vegetables provided substance and variety for home consumption.[4]

1. St. Augustine *News*, September 11, 1840; St. Augustine *Florida Herald,* April 10, 1843.    2. Latrobe, *The Rambler in North America,* II, 31.
3. Williams, "Florida in the Union," p. 121.
4. Martin, *Florida During Territorial Days,* pp. 110-17.

58

Still, the problems posed by a new area and the vagaries of its climate and soil added to the usual concerns faced by others of their occupation elsewhere. Few of them probably believed that political action would solve all their ills; rather it was resentment which appears to have dictated the movement of so many of them into the Democratic fold—resentment against special privilege, resentment of control of *their* government by a privileged few, and resentment of the banks not only because of the inconveniences bank management produced, but also because bank operation provided little opportunity for members of their class to acquire any or additional slaves.

Higher up in the agricultural ladder were the small and large planters. Most of the large plantations were in Middle Florida, the area between the Suwannee and the Apalachicola rivers comprising the counties of Leon, Gadsden, Jefferson, Madison, and Hamilton. The first three of these counties, together with Jackson which lay immediately west of the Apalachicola, composed the cotton belt of the territory. By 1838 these four counties alone accounted for the bulk of the territorial wealth. Short-staple cotton, tobacco, and sugar cane were the main crops, although cotton ranked first and accounted by 1840 for 80 per cent of Florida's 30,000 bales.[5] In many respects this region closely resembled the Alabama Black Belt and the Georgia Piedmont. The economic and political hub of this little world was Leon County, which held within its borders a larger number of slaves than any other county in the territory. The wealthier plantations averaged between 1,500 and 2,500 acres and held from thirty to forty-five slaves. A few ran up to 10,000 acres and over one hundred slaves, with two estates confining well over three hundred each.[6]

By no means were all of these "aristocrats" particularly aristocratic in their behavior. In many instances it was difficult to differentiate one of them from the more common variety of Caucasian without first checking his bank connections.[7] A large percentage of them were, of course, tied to the Union Bank of Tallahassee, and many of their possessions stemmed from its extremely favorable policies during the 1830's. There were a few, however, in Leon and

5. Dodd, *Florida Becomes a State*, p. 36.
6. Julia Hering, "Plantation Economy in Leon County, 1830-1840," *Florida Historical Quarterly*, XXXIII (July, 1954), 32, 34, 36-38; microfilm copies of the original schedules of the United States Census for Florida, 1840.
7. Benwell, *An Englishman's Travels in America*, pp. 170-171.

Jefferson counties who were not a part of the Bank-Whig circle. They resented the unfair and additional competition induced by the bank's largess. It was no accident, therefore, that this small minority of large Middle Florida planters also moved into the Democratic party. On the other hand, it is the author's impression, based on a statistical breakdown of the Democratic leadership, that a far greater number of the small planters were swelling the Democratic ranks.[8] Unfortunately, since small plantations were fairly well distributed and interspersed with the larger estates, county voting records do not reveal the extent of their owners' refusal to join the ranks of the Whigs. Though it is quite possible that only a minority of these small planters joined the Democrats, still their number probably exceeded that in the older and more settled regions of the South.

Another group which seems to have cast a considerable proportion of its political weight with the Democratic party was composed of the territory's business elements—the merchants, the rural capitalists, and the village entrepreneurs. Here again some significant qualifications must be made, particularly in the case of the merchants and shippers. Regional differences and competition with nearby ports were often influential factors which transcended party battles. The East Florida ports of Jacksonville and St. Augustine, for example, were rarely on friendly terms.[9] The competition was even more bitter between Apalachicola and St. Joseph in West Florida.[10] Each of the four ports displayed such strong animosity toward the other located in the same area that occasionally each was successful in securing the election of a candidate of the opposing party.

In Franklin County's Apalachicola the wealthier interests also stood by the banks and supported George T. Ward against Levy in both 1841 and 1843. They boasted that their town alone paid more taxes than all the East Florida counties combined. It should be noted, too, that they exported 100,000 bales of cotton—more than three times that produced in the entire territory. Obviously, most of it came down the Apalachicola River from connecting rivers in the southeastern Alabama and southwestern Georgia plantation areas.

8. Following the lead of others, this writer bases his arbitrary distinctions on the following figures: yeoman, 0-5 slaves; small planter, 6-50; large planter, over 50.

9. St. Augustine *Florida Herald*, May 5, 1838.

10. St. Joseph *Times*, June 1, 1839.

This, plus the existence of a branch of the Union Bank, gave the local economic elite a strong Whig complexion.[11] Indeed, Governor Reid, as well as Westcott, Levy, Walker Anderson, Thomas Baltzell, and Leigh Read—the major Democratic leaders—were scurrilously denounced as "adventurers," "loafers," "demagogues," "agitators," and "office hunters," "without property, standing or character."[12]

Calhoun County's younger merchants in the rising port of St. Joseph sang a different tune. Criticizing the Union Bank, they insisted that, "The Florida merchants have been miserably imposed upon, by the great loss they are compelled to sustain in making satisfactory remittances to the North."[13] They also vented their spleen against the planter of Leon County who "established at the seat of government, surrounded by a wealthy high-toned and chivalric population is yet insensible to the dictates of a liberal policy —and with the mistaken and bigoted zeal of the Frenchman, who looks upon 'Paris as France, and France as the World,' has worked himself into the belief, that Tallahassee is Florida!"[14] The agitation they managed to create also produced from 1839 on an annual Democratic representative to the Council.

Perhaps more significant was the cleavage within the business community which arose from the differences between a few really wealthy, well-established merchants and a larger number of newer entrepreneurs of more modest means. These intra-community conflicts were often exceedingly important in drawing local political lines. In St. Augustine Moses Elias Levy, prominent importer and large land speculator, not only supported the Whigs, but also provided them with considerable ammunition when he denounced the political activities of his son David.[15] In Tallahassee the very wealthiest businessmen, such as R. A. Shine, were intimately tied to the "Large Planter-Bank-Whig Axis," while their lesser counterparts joined the Democratic party.[16]

In general, therefore, the Jacksonians could count on the support of the smaller merchants, manufacturers, warehousemen, retailers, and operators of grist mills, saw mills, and foundries. In addition,

11. Apalachicola *Florida Journal,* March 24, 1841.
12. St. Augustine *Florida Herald,* September 12, 1840.
13. St. Joseph *Times,* September 17, 1839.
14. *Ibid.,* August 1, 1838.
15. Thompson, "David L. Yulee," pp. 8, 24; M. E. Levy to D. Levy, November 6, 1842 (Yulee Papers).
16. St. Joseph *Times,* September 17, 1839; Tallahassee *Floridian,* March 28, 1840.

61

the self-employed petty entrepreneurs developed a very strong affinity for the Democratic position. Among them were included a large number of printers, carpenters, blacksmiths, wainwrights, masons, tailors, boot and shoe makers, cabinet makers, metalsmiths and fishermen—those referred to as the "artisans," "mechanics" and "workingmen."[17]

Finally, there was "labor," those for the most part who were not property owners but were employed by others for wages. A surprisingly large percentage of this category, particularly in manufacturing, trade, and commerce, were slaves or free Negroes. Even by the 1850's the free white laboring force was still of negligible size.[18] Among the whites, however, the overseers and journeymen mechanics were probably the most significant. During this early era of partisan activity they appear to have pursued a fluctuating political course. The political and social ideas of the Democratic party were appealing, but the journeymen as employees of the merchants, manufacturers, and artisans also wanted higher wages, a more stable currency, and a labor lien law. As a consequence, many of them fell prey to Whig appeals. Protest meetings of the journeymen mechanics were held occasionally, and some of them even joined in a defense of the bank against the merchants and mechanics.[19] But the Whigs did nothing for them and by the mid-forties more and more of these people seem to have gravitated to the Democrats.[20] Indeed in May, 1845, a five-man Committee of Overseers and Mechanics of Leon County addressed letters to candidates of both parties asking their position on a lien law. It was significant and typical of the new political order that both Whigs and Democrats replied, and all of their responses were favorable.[21] But it was even more significant that neither party actually did anything about it.

If it has been difficult to achieve any degree of accuracy in ascertaining who actually voted for the Democratic party, it is possible to establish with some exactness the character and content of

17. Thompson, "David L. Yulee," pp. 14-15; Dodd, "Florida in 1845," *Florida Historical Quarterly*, XXIV (July, 1945), 10.

18. Thompson, "Political Nativism in Florida, 1848-1860," *Journal of Southern History*, XV (February, 1949), 54.

19. St. Augustine *Florida Herald*, October 6, 1838; Quincy *Sentinel*, October 9, 1840; Tallahassee *Floridian*, April 10, 1841.

20. Tallahassee *Floridian*, October 10, 1840; Tallahassee *Star of Florida*, September 6, 1844, September 26, 1845.

21. Tallahassee *Star of Florida*, May 23, 1845.

its leadership. Even here, however, there are limits. Among those factors lending a measure of imprecision to the subsequent analysis are the following: personal fortunes often fluctuated, as did individual occupations; a certain amount of intra-territorial migration took place; except for a hard core, there was considerable turnover among local leaders; and both inaccurate and often incomplete returns mar the national census figures. Since the Florida manuscript schedules of the 1840 census have been a prime source for this study of the Jacksonians, the last qualification noted should be clarified. Some persons arrived after the census was taken; others were displaced as a result of the Seminole War. Some individuals were omitted because they were on a trip or they were never located; others—including militiamen, journeymen, and a variety of boarders—were usually added to the total of a particular household or of a military command in the field. Especially exasperating were those instances where important information about a listed individual was simply omitted. In at least two cases prominent Democratic county census takers, though signing their census returns, failed to include data on themselves. Despite these shortcomings, the manuscript census schedules, together with a host of personal papers, government documents, and newspapers, provide a good portrait of the Jacksonian Democratic leadership in Florida.

From an assorted number of sources, an impressive list of 150 leaders was compiled. On the list were candidates for local, county, territorial, and national offices who ran on the Democratic ticket between 1839 and 1845. Eliminating duplications, officers of and delegates to county, district, and territorial party meetings and conventions were added. Those individuals who served in a variety of official organizational capacities were also included, among them members of resolutions, nominating, correspondence, and reception committees. Analysis of the data on these Jacksonians produces the following composite.

The relatively high degree of youthfulness is revealing; 67 per cent were in their twenties and thirties; specifically, 21 per cent in their twenties; 46 per cent, thirties; 27 per cent, forties; 5 per cent, fifties; and 1 per cent, sixties.[22] The Whigs were not unaware of this tendency and attempted to exploit it. In one instance they castigated a Democratic leader: "Mr. Westcott need not have told

22. The Florida manuscript schedules for the Sixth Census of 1840 merely list ages by decade categories. See Table 4.

the world that he was a youth—but he might have said that he always would be one, and green at that."[23]

It is extremely unfortunate that information on wealth and property ownership was not solicited in the 1840 survey. They were included in the next decennial census, but the situation in the intervening period was too fluid to permit the use of those figures at this point with any degree of validity. On the other hand, slaveholding statistics *are* available. Since slaveholding was a fairly reliable index to the agricultural scene and since an overwhelming majority of the varied types of businessmen in towns utilized slave labor, these figures are significant. Of the 130 Democratic leaders for whom slave figures are available, only 26, or 20 per cent, held no slaves at all. The great majority of these nonslaveholders fell into the yeoman and professional classifications. Still, with 80 per cent being slaveowners, and over 70 per cent of that number holding more than five slaves, one must conclude that these men constituted a reasonably well-to-do band of leaders.[24]

An occupational breakdown of these Jacksonians confirms the already suggested amorphous middle-class nature of the movement. The distribution, however, is skewed toward the professional and somewhat wealthier elements in the society. The small planters, comprising 30 per cent of the leadership, constituted the largest single group. The professionals, consisting mainly of lawyers, were disproportionately influential as compared with their number in the territory. They were second in size, with 23 per cent, but they were also among the most active. On the other hand, yeomen accounted for only 14 per cent of the leaders, which was undoubtedly considerably less than the group's contribution on election day. The figures for all groups are: small planters, 30 per cent; professionals, 23 per cent; manufacturers and traders (including self-employed artisans), 18 per cent; yeomen, 14 per cent; men of commerce, 8 per cent; large planters, 7 per cent.[25] Note should be made here that a sizeable number, at least 10 per cent, engaged in multiple economic pursuits. Most of them were small planters and were listed as such, since that was their primary activity. However, they participated also in nonagricultural fields, with the result that the leading category might well be adjusted downward and some of the others correspondingly upward.

23. Tallahassee *Florida Sentinel*, November 5, 1841.
24. See Table 5.    25. See Table 6.

These, then, were the Democratic leaders. In many ways they were a diverse lot, more so perhaps than the Whig leaders. They included in their ranks a few large, irate, antibank planters; a larger number of insecure small planters; an expanding group of struggling businessmen; a number of forthright yeoman farmers; a considerable contingent of eager professional persons; and a small core of shrewd political entrepreneurs. Each group had its own problems and each individual had his own aspirations. Regardess of these apparent differences, most of them were alike in that they were enterprising young men "on the make." They all shared a common resentment against the existing order and were determined to alter some, but by no means all, aspects of the status quo. In this the Democratic leadership struck a responsive chord in the electorate.

In summarizing the political sentiment of the diverse Jacksonians, therefore, it may be stated with a reasonable degree of certainty that the Democratic revolt was primarily a middle-class movement —middle class in the nineteenth-century sense of that term—of the lesser, independent, property-holding groups. And, contrary to Whig apprehensions, it was certainly no lower-class manifestation of radicalism. Rather, as has been suggested earlier, it was almost exclusively a struggle to broaden the base of economic and political opportunity.

# 6. REACTION AND REVIVAL

The rise of the Democratic party in territorial Florida came as a shock to the existing elite. The shock soon turned to anger, which assumed a variety of forms, including occasional violence. Ultimately, of course, those who became Whigs calmed their nerves, consolidated their ranks, emulated many of the Democratic party techniques, and managed to enjoy a brief revival.

The initial response to the introduction of parties into their midst, however, revealed more than dismay. The existence of factions was condemned, their importance disavowed, and calls were issued for a vote which transcended any class differences. One group solemnly opposed "any attempt to array any one class of our citizens against another." "Let us vote," they urged, "not in platoons, by trades, but as men having common interests." Another group announced, "We are of no party but the Florida party." Friends and neighbors were to cooperate for the benefit of the entire community.[1] Other groups were less facile in concealing their disdain. They believed that the Whigs were much too refined to "dabble in the dirty puddle of partisan politics," and their adherence to justice, truth, and immutable principles would be shaken neither "by the chances of a petty election" nor by "croaking politicians."[2] The conservatives were conscious of the Democratic party's objectives and were equally cognizant of the class content which shaped those objectives. They repeatedly denounced those who would promote class distinctions or "set the poor against the rich," likening them to "Jacobins," "Levellers," and "radicals." In the heat of debate a few went to extremes, revealing their deeper aristocratic feelings and fears. And now, they mocked, "we are to have a Social Democracy! . . . Men of education, throw open your doors and your hearts to the illiterate, boorish and savage. Men of taste and refinement, consort indiscriminately with the vulgar—men of morals with the profane; men of sense with the blockheads."[3]

1. St. Joseph *Times*, October 1, 1839; Pensacola *Gazette*, October 6, 1838; Tallahassee *Florida Sentinel*, September 5, 1843.
2. Tallahassee *Florida Sentinel*, November 5, 1841; Tallahassee *Star of Florida*, October 20, 1841; St. Joseph *Times*, August 21, 1840.
3. Thompson, "David L. Yulee," pp. 16-17; St. Augustine *News*, May 8, 1840; Quincy *Sentinel*, December 25, 1840.

When the first shock had subsided, calmer minds prevailed. On the issue of the banks, for example, there were some who acknowledged that these institutions had indeed been mismanaged. But let's use the banks properly, they cried, not break them![4] The use of the term "democratic" by their opponents was also of concern to the rising Whig party. What's in a name? "Much," they moaned, and "in this case more than much. *Mark what we say*—The party that wears this name exclusively can't be beat. The term *democracy*, as it indicates, is the exponent of popular rights, and will forever, all the world over, carry with it a force which no power can permanently resist. . . . We are out of all patience with those of our Whig brethren who continue to allow the Locofocos the name of *Democrats.*"[5] A number of newspapers, including the Quincy *Sentinel* and the St. Augustine *News*, insisted that their candidates represented the "true Democratic Republican ticket." The opposition was little more than Loco-Focos, Federals, or even Federal Loco-Focos.[6] Later, in desperation, these leaders termed one of their nominees the "American candidate" and hoisted his name over a crossed flag and bald eagle bearing the slogan "Our Country."[7]

Expressions of differences, however, were not confined to the more peaceful methods of debate, slogan, and invective during the initial phase of the Democratic ascendancy. Though not the usual form, political violence did occur frequently enough during 1839 and 1840 to justify its inclusion here as an opposition technique. In October, 1839, for example, Leigh Read was contesting the Council seat of a Leon County bank man. Political discussion between the two degenerated into a personal quarrel, and the Conservative challenged his opponent to a duel. Consistent with his stand at the constitutional convention, Read ignored the challenge. He also ignored that of his adversary's second. Then, when the campaign had become nothing more than a series of riots and armed parties of belligerents repeatedly parading through the streets of Tallahassee, Read reluctantly agreed to meet his opponent's second, Colonel Augustus Alston, a former director of the Union Bank.

4. St. Joseph *Times*, April 1, 1840.

5. St. Augustine *News*, October 29, 1842.

6. "Loco-foco" was a term of opprobrium applied to the Democrats between 1838 and 1845. Many of them, particularly the Jacksonians of East Florida, accepted it as the badge of their Democracy.

7. St. Augustine *News*, August 7, 1840, October and November, 1842, April and May, 1843. Reference is to George T. Ward in the 1843 delegate race.

They fought with weapons and on terms set down by Alston, who was promptly killed on the first try.[8] In the Democratic upsurge of the day, Leigh Read went on to victory, but the affair had not ended by any means.

On the Sunday evening prior to the opening of the new Legislative Council session in January, 1840, about one hundred persons were quietly having dinner at the capital's Adelphi Hotel. Among the Democrats present conversation centered on the impending bank conflict and the probable selection of Read as speaker of the lower house. The general quiet of the dinner hour was interrupted when Willis Alston, brother of the late Augustus, shot and stabbed Read. Read survived and was elected speaker, an honor which he declined in favor of recuperating from his wounds. In the meantime an inflamed and frustrated Alston made further threats against Read and other Democrats, including Governor Reid who deplored the assault in his message to the legislature.[9] Alston escaped, but he would return.

Perhaps the most serious eruption of party lawlessness took place in August, 1840. The crisis in this instance was precipitated by one of the resolutions of a Leon County Democratic meeting on July 30. The offensive statement resolved party opposition to "the recent union between the bank party of this territory and the abolitionists . . . of the north."[10] Abolitionists, indeed! This was going too far. When the resolutions appeared in the Democratic *Floridian* of August 1, a Whig group descended on the newspaper office, threatened its editor, Samuel Sibley, and demanded the name of the author. A St. Augustine *News* reporter stated later that "we then threatened if he did not, his office must come down." Sibley stalled any violence temporarily by promising to secure the information. Walker Anderson then saved Sibley by professing authorship of the offending resolution. At about the same time Willis Alston, who had escaped to Texas after his assault on General Read, returned to Tallahassee. Personal hatred combined with party conflict and almost turned the town into a battlefield. On August 3 the "Bowie Knife Knights" whooped through the streets "screaming vengeance against the d — d loco-focos." Alston and a group of bitter Whig partisans attacked William H. Francis, a prominent merchant and Democrat. They abused him and provoked a street brawl. Walker

8. St. Augustine *Florida Herald*, September 12, 1840.
9. *Ibid.*, September 12, 19, 1840; *House Journal* (1840), pp. 9, 17-18.
10. Tallahassee *Floridian*, August 1, September 19, 1840.

Anderson, chairman of the House Judiciary Committee in 1840, which had reported against the banks, was also attacked as he walked down the street. "A Whig director of the Union Bank was standing by this party of hectoring bullies" as Anderson was threatened with pistols and knives. Thomas S. Brown, who had served as secretary to the now famous 1840 House Investigating Committee on Banking, albeit as a states' rights, antibank Whig, was the next victim. In front of the Adelphi Hotel he was threatened with lynching if he failed to leave town.[11]

The hectic events of August 3 prompted Governor Reid to call up a nearby militia group the following day. A disgruntled bank group, furious with this display of "military despotism," descended on the capitol, broke into the governor's office, and demanded an explanation. Reid reminded them that the use of the militia was not uncommon and, besides, it was in town only to keep the peace. The strong stand of the governor forced the protestants to withdraw, and they retreated to a local bar where they revived their spirits. That evening they devoted themselves to provoking the militiamen who, under orders from Reid, ignored their taunts.[12]

On August 5 the troops were withdrawn. Within a week Reid wrote to Poinsett defending his action as necessary to preserve order. The activities of the Union Bank and the return of Alston, he observed, had caused a serious breach of the peace.[13] He later addressed a similar letter to Secretary of State John Forsyth.[14] But the Whigs protested to Van Buren, denouncing Reid's action as a desecration of free soil and calling for the governor's removal.[15]

But the August days of lawlessness had not yet run their course. On the sixteenth another group of Whigs, again armed with pistols and knives, attacked Elias E. Blackburn while he was in Tallahassee on business. The Jefferson County Democratic leader suffered a sound beating. During the same day David M. Sheffield, who had signed a Democratic resolution defending Reid against the Whig bankites, was literally bludgeoned by R. B. Copeland, former private secretary to ex-Governor Call.[16] The response of the Demo-

11. Tallahassee *Floridian*, September 19, 1840; St. Augustine *Florida Herald*, September 18, 1840.

12. St. Augustine *Florida Herald*, September 18, 1840.

13. R. R. Reid to J. R. Poinsett, August 12, 1840 (Historical Society of Pennsylvania).

14. R. R. Reid to J. Forsyth, December 10, 1840, "R. R. Reid Letterbook."

15. Tallahassee *Floridian*, August 15, 1840; St. Augustine *News*, August 28, September 4, 1840.     16. St. Augustine *Florida Herald*, September 19, 1840.

cratic leaders and press to these events hardly needs much review. The St. Joseph *Times,* on the other hand, soberly warned its Whig friends: "The papers at Tallahassee, more than confirmed by private reports, show a disturbed state of society in Leon County, partaking of a personal and party character. . . . Violence and proscription are not the best tests of sincerity and honesty of purpose. . . . Pistols, Bowie Knives and Bludgeons may frighten slaves, but cannot intimidate freemen."[17]

A rather melodramatic end to the entire episode came in April of the following year. In June, 1840, when Leigh Read had recovered from his wounds, Van Buren appointed him marshal of Middle Florida. Fortunately or unfortunately, as the case may be, Read was at West Point as a Visitor when Willis Alston returned to Tallahassee that summer. Their paths finally crossed on April 26, 1841, when Alston, on still another return visit, stepped from a hidden doorway and blasted Read with a double-barreled shotgun. This time Alston's efforts were rewarded; this time he was also captured. But when the county judge refused to allow the murderer's release on bail, two former county judges forced that justice to let them sit with him and then promptly granted bail by a vote of two to one. Thus, Alston's political ties proved beneficial and he escaped once more.[18]

Let it be said here that the majority of the Conservatives and their successors, the Whigs, probably condemned this resort to violence. But it is clear that there were some among the ostensibly well-bred, aristocratic bank elite of Middle Florida who were willing either to resort to violence themselves or to acquiesce in its use by some of their supporters. By and large, however, the Democrats' opponents confined their reactions to more peaceful channels. They condemned the patronage system and what they referred to as the loco-foco drive to control all territorial offices.[19] They ridiculed the Democratic appeals to the people as well as the ignorance and illiteracy of their opponents.[20] They utilized whatever legislative methods they were familiar with to frustrate Democratic majorities, including taking over the organization of the lower house in 1841

17. September 4, 1840.
18. Tallahassee *Floridian,* June 6, 1840, May 1, 1841; St. Augustine *Florida Herald,* September 12, 1840, June 25, 1841; R. R. Reid's diary entry, April 28, 1841, in Miller, *Bench and Bar in Georgia,* II, 226.
19. St. Augustine *News,* June 18, 1841.
20. Quincy *Sentinel,* July 24, 1840.

when many of the Democrats, who had a majority, had not yet arrived from remote frontier East Florida.[21] And, they could rationalize the election of a Democrat by suggesting that the victor was "a man who will not suffer politics, or rather party ties, to sway him in his legislative course."[22]

There were other factors, too, which aided the Whig cause and paved the way for the Democratic reversals in the fall elections of 1842 and 1843. Paradoxically, the Panic of 1837, which contributed to a national Whig victory, led to the triumph of the Jacksonian Democrats in Florida. But William Henry Harrison's term, brief as it was, gave life to the Florida Whigs. Many of the Jackson men of early territorial days had supported Harrison in 1840. Among them could be counted the first three civil governors: William P. DuVal, John H. Eaton, and Richard K. Call.[23] The consequence of Call's support and Harrison's victory was all too evident to Robert Raymond Reid. He recorded in his dairy on March 29, 1841, "reports of my dismissal from office not confirmed by the papers, but it will come." And four days later, "I am preparing for the ejection. I expect the old hero will certainly send me *packing*."[24] On April 3 news finally reached Reid that he had been removed.[25] His predecessor had become his successor. The return of Call gave considerable impetus to his party's development, and Harrison's death provided little relief for the Democrats. He had lived long enough to reappoint Call and the damage had been done. Tyler, though admitting to David Levy that Call would not have been his selection, did nothing to alter the situation.[26]

By the summer of that same year one of the worst yellow-fever epidemics in Florida's history brought further woes to the Democrats. Though the disease failed to display any class or political partisanship, it did count Robert Reid and two successive editors of the *Floridian* among its victims.[27]

Probably the most devastating blow to the Democrats stemmed from the Whigs' emulation of Democratic techniques. The Whigs

21. St. Augustine *Florida Herald*, February 5, 1841.
22. Tallahassee *Florida Sentinel*, November 18, 1842.
23. Doherty, "Richard Keith Call," p. 232. Eaton of course had left Florida in 1836.    24. Miller, *Bench and Bar in Georgia*, II, 225.
25. C. Downing to R. K. Call, March 8, 1841 (Call Papers, Florida Historical Society Library).
26. D. Levy to J. D. Westcott, Jr., May 6, 1842 (copy, Yulee Papers).
27. Tallahassee *Floridian*, July 10, September 11, 25, 1841. The editors were Edward R. Gibson and Nathaniel M. Hibbard.

71

too were getting out and addressing "the people"; they too were starting their own organizational drive; and they too were beginning to hold their own nominating conventions.[28]

The Democrats still cried, "To the Polls! To the Polls! Democrats, vote early! Let every man bring his neighbor."[29] But now the Whigs were making their contribution to the color, chaos, and confusion of election day. A northern observer depicted the 1843 canvass in St. Augustine as one in which "fighting, swearing & drinking . . . were served up in abundance & almost made one blush at such a specimen of republicanism."[30]

Still other factors undermined the Democratic cause. The Whigs were fully aware that the bank stand of their earlier candidates had hurt them, and they began to soft-pedal the issue. Moreover, Richard Call, though still refusing to repudiate the faith bonds, did resist the pressure of foreign bondholders. He insisted that the territorial government was nothing more than "a remote and contingent endorser" and his stand undoubtedly encouraged many taxpayers.[31] In addition, some Whig organizations carefully refrained from the use of that party designation, referring instead to their group of candidates as the antibank, antibond, and antistate "Peoples' Ticket."[32]

The cumulative effect of all these reverses and new Whig activities hurt the Democrats in the elections for the Legislative Council of 1843 and 1844. The lower house of 1843, for example, was the only one between 1839 and 1845 in which a majority of the counties did not have Democratic representatives. Worse still for the Democrats, the Whigs had for the first time gained majorities in both houses of the legislature. Now the Whigs celebrated and their victory barbecues spotted the countryside.[33] The 1843 poll improved the democratic situation slightly, but the Whigs continued in control of the Senate and retained a working majority in the House.[34] Actually, when the legislators elected late in 1843 met in 1844, the Democrats held some hope of at least regaining control of the lower house. They caucused on January 1 and nominated Wakulla Coun-

28. Tallahassee *Florida Sentinel*, September 20, 1842, July 18, August 1, 22, 1843; Tallahassee *Star of Florida*, August 16, 30, 1844.
29. St. Augustine *Florida Herald*, November 7, 1843.
30. *Bishop Whipple's Southern Diary*, pp. 22-23.
31. Doherty, "Richard Keith Call." pp. 241, 244.
32. St. Augustine *News*, July 30, November 12, 1842, October 12, 1844.
33. St. Augustine *News*, November 12, 1842.
34. See tables 1 and 2.

ty's Nathaniel W. Walker for speaker. But on January 4 Duval County's perennial Whig representative, Joseph B. Lancaster, was elected with the aid of some moderate Democrats.[35] In 1843 and 1844 the Whig-controlled sessions produced no major legislation, though the nominal Democratic lower-house majority did produce some friction with Governor Call in 1844. Resentful of their political decline, the Democrats piously turned from patronage and sought to increase the number of elective offices, including territorial auditor, treasurer, and many justices of the peace. The attempt failed when some of their number crossed party lines.[36]

During this initial Whig ascendancy, the major standing issues centering on statehood and the banks were resolved in a fashion which could not have been predicted by the delegates to the St. Joseph convention in 1838. The banking functions of the Union Bank of Tallahassee were suspended until it was able to resume specie payments.[37] Indeed, many Democrats must have been rudely roused from their legislative slumbers as they heard Call's message criticize "the incorporation of banking companies, without capital, and with the extraordinary privilege of raising millions of money on the faith and responsibility of the Territory."[38] In addition, the Whig forces had, paradoxically, become identified with the antistatehood position. Many of them joined with a group of like-minded East Florida Democrats and adopted a series of resolutions opposing statehood until the people voted on the issue again, and favoring the division of Florida into two separate territories.[39]

Times had indeed changed. The creation of a two-party system and the pressures it had produced in the pursuit of votes had wrought some rather remarkable shifts in policy. There would soon be other reversals, among them the revival of Democratic political fortunes. Despite the Democratic defeats in the fall of 1842 and 1843, the thread of continuity which gave them their greatest hope for a revival was the re-election of David Levy in May, 1843.

The drive to return Levy to Congress illustrated once more the effectiveness of the varied party techniques the Democrats had introduced earlier. Conventions in Tallahassee, St. Augustine, Palatka,

35. Tallahassee *Florida Sentinel*, January 2, 1844; *House Journal* (1844), p. 7.
36. Tallahassee *Florida Sentinel*, February 13, March 19, 1844.
37. *Acts and Resolutions of the Legislative Council* (1843), pp. 59-62.
38. *House Journal* (1843), p. 10.
39. *Acts and Resolutions of the Legislative Council* (1843), p. 66, (1844), pp. 95-96.

Newnansville, and other communities in the territory resulted in enthusiastic and largely unanimous nominations of Levy.[40] The St. Augustine Democratic Party Resolutions Committee reluctantly subscribed to "the republican principle of rotation in office," but insisted at its meeting on March 4 that Levy had the strongest claim to the position. The delegate's accomplishments and near-accomplishments were carefully, completely, and compellingly spread through all districts. Appropriations for roads, bridges, river improvements, lighthouses, fortifications including the Pensacola Navy Yard—all had their particular local appeals. Securing $800,000 with which the Florida volunteer militia could finally be paid just before the election, however, was an example of either masterful timing or extraordinary coincidence.[41] In any case, it proved to have considerable public appeal. Vigorous "exertions made by the Locos," the establishment of special newspapers to advocate the delegate's re-election, the promise of continued postmasterships from Charles Wickliffe, and the widespread affection accorded the hard-working candidate—and opponent George T. Ward's persistent defense of the bank position—all these contributed to Levy's victory.[42]

Further impetus to the Democratic advance came the following summer. Richard K. Call's term as governor came to an end in July, 1844. President Tyler, in large measure because of Levy's constant pressure, passed over Call and appointed John Branch, a Democrat. The Democrats once more had control of both the governor's and the delegate's offices. There remained only the task of recapturing the Legislative Council. Once again David Levy played a key role.

By 1844 Iowa was ready for admission to the Union. But the national acceptance of a kind "of compromise at this stage of intersectional relations" which called for the simultaneous admission of a northern and southern territory provided Levy with the needed opportunity.[43] Levy, Westcott, and the other Democratic leaders who favored statehood recognized that the application of Iowa afforded the most propitious opportunity for the creation of a state of

40. St. Augustine *Florida Herald*, March 13, 1843.

41. *Ibid.*; St. Augustine *News*, May 20, 1843.

42. St. Augustine *News*, May 20, 1843; Pensacola *Gazette*, April 8, 1843; Apalachicola *Commercial Advertiser*, February 25, 1843; Washington *Globe*, May 22, 1843; see Table 3.

43. Franklin A. Doty, "Florida, Iowa, and the National Balance of Power, 1845," *Florida Historical Quarterly*, XXXV (July, 1956), 52.

Florida since its first petition in 1839.[44] For three years Levy had quietly worked for admission, but now his efforts exploded into the effective *Circular Letter*.[45] The banks were no longer at issue; now statehood would advance the "great principles of Democracy."[46] Capitalizing on the antistatehood stand of the Whigs at the previous two sessions of the Legislative Council, and probably aided by the influx in 1843 of more state-conscious immigrants under the Armed Occupation Act, the Democrats regained control of both houses of the Council in the fall elections of 1844. They were victorious in a majority of both East and Middle Florida county races for the House. In the fight for the Senate they swept the entire Middle Florida slate, but the persistence of division sentiment and the presence of better known Whig candidates gave a majority of the counties to the opposition in East Florida.[47] In any event, the Democratic triple triumph of the early forties which included control of governor, delegate, and Legislative Council was restored.

The presidential election added further strength to the local Democratic revival.[48] Polk's victory was celebrated from St. Augustine to Pensacola, while some Whigs protested the partisan joy exuded even by federal officeholders.[49] The enthusiasm generated by the national and territorial party victories in November, the actual petition of Iowa to Congress for admission in December, and the mounting pressure from Levy made statehood the dominant issue in the Legislative Council of 1845.[50]

The success of the Democrats at that session, and more significantly the action of the national government, also made it the last meeting of the Council. In Tallahassee an almost straight party division carried a statehood resolution 26 to 6 in the House and 9 to 6 in the Senate. The six opposition votes in the Senate were all Whig, three each from East and West Florida. In the lower chamber five of the six negative votes were from East Florida, the other from West Florida; three were Whigs, one an independent, and two of questionable party affiliation.[51] Despite the fact that eight of the

44. *Congressional Globe*, 28th Congress, 2nd Session, pp. 275, 283-86.
45. See above, p 38.    46. St. Augustine *Florida Herald*, June 18, 1844.
47. See tables 1 and 2.
48. Apalachicola *Commercial Advertiser*, June 15, 1844.
49. St. Augustine *News*, November 23, December 21, 1844.
50. Thompson, "David L. Yulee," p. 29; Doty, "Florida, Iowa, and the National Balance of Power, 1845," p. 41.
51. St. Augustine *News*, February 8, 1845; *House Journal* (1845), p. 52; *Senate Journal* (1845), p. 69.

twelve votes cast against statehood came from East Florida, the legislature's Democratic leadership came from that region. William A. Forward, Levy's ally and subsequent business associate from St. Johns County, was House speaker, and George W. Macrae, representing Dade and Monroe counties, was Senate president. Together with Middle Florida's Westcott, they carried the day for admission.[52] By the beginning of February they were apprehensive lest Congress fail in *its* contribution, but national events and Levy were moving in their favor. The House of Representatives approved statehood for Iowa and Florida on February 13, the Senate followed suit on March 1, and Tyler signed the bill into law two days later.[53]

While the Democrats rejoiced in their latest triumph, their leaders were already laying the groundwork for the coming state elections. A constant flow of letters streamed back and forth between Levy in Washington and the leaders in Florida. Levy rejected Westcott's suggestion that he come to Tallahassee for a general party conclave. He urged instead that Democratic members of the legislature go back to their respective districts after adjournment, "there to remain in the field rallying & animating the people till the day of election."[54] The question of candidates also arose, even before Senate approval of statehood. For the General Assembly reliable local selections would suffice. But what of governor and representative to Congress? Levy, Westcott, and Walker Anderson were agreed that one of the two posts should certainly go to Middle Florida. Levy assumed that they would run John Branch for governor; if not, he recommended William Bailey, prominent Jefferson County planter. He disputed Westcott's contention that the Whigs might capture the Assembly and countered by sending his own estimate of the first assembly's political complexion. The specific county-by-county analysis, assigning a Democratic majority to both houses, proved to be incredibly accurate.[55]

But all this was idle speculation, Levy maintained, unless their party adopted the proper procedures. More leadership was to be mobilized in the respective districts of the new state. Westcott was

52. Though exceedingly influential, Westcott was not a member of the Council at this time. The party division should not obscure the fact that Richard Call was a considerable force in the statehood movement.

53. *Niles' Weekly Register*, March 29, 1845; Iowa, of course, was not actually admitted until December, 1846.

54. D. Levy to J. D. Westcott, Jr., February 22, 1845 (copy, Yulee Papers).

55. D. Levy to J. D. Westcott, Jr. and W. Anderson, March 7, 1845 (Manuscript Division, Duke University Library).

"to take hold" in his area; Anderson was to get George S. Hawkins, Chandler C. Yonge, Robert Myers, and Robert J. Floyd "into the field" in the West where the Democrats were weakest; Levy himself would return to the East and work with William A. Forward. "Let every man," he ordered, "who seeks preferment from the state, or Mr. Polk's admn. show their desert by service in this great election." By all means, he agreed, have a state convention, and he added, "Let a good address be prepared & printed in advance, so that it can be distributed by the members of the convention. Whatever expenses are necessary for this or other means of reaching the people, assess me for my share."[56]

By early April Levy was back in Florida. Whether illness, as he claimed, or political strategy kept him from attending the first state Democratic convention cannot be ascertained. His absence did spare him some intramural disagreements, and in the end he achieved what he wanted. The party convention met at Madison Court House on April 14 and 15. Again temporary chairman and secretary, permanent chairman and secretaries, three vice-presidents —one from each district—and a rules committee composed of one from each county gave a sizeable number of delegates a sense of importance and participation. The major conflict of the two-day meeting erupted over the question of the number of convention votes and how they were to be apportioned among the several districts and counties for the purpose of selecting their two state-wide candidates. The matter was resolved by assigning a satisfactory number of specific votes to each county. The convention was then ready to select its candidates. Joseph Branch nominated David Levy for representative to Congress and he promptly won by acclamation. The choice was undoubtedly facilitated by Levy's previous correspondence with Westcott on the subject and the notification of his county's delegation that he would run if selected.[57] With Levy on the ticket, the choice of governor had to come from Middle Florida. William D. Moseley, William Bailey, and Robert Butler went through two ballots before Moseley received a unanimous vote.[58]

The superior Democratic organization and the forceful planning of Levy now bore fruit. By mid-April of 1845 the Democrats had had their convention and their candidates were ready for action.

56. *Ibid.;* D. Levy to J. D. Westcott, Jr., March 21, 1845 (copy, Yulee Papers).
57. D. Levy to J. D. Westcott, Jr., April 13, 1845 (copy, Yulee Papers).
58. St. Augustine *News,* April 19, 26, 1845.

The Whigs had done virtually nothing, and it was too late to make plans for a regular convention. Only an informal meeting of some Middle Florida leaders on April 22 provided them with Richard K. Call and East Florida's Benjamin A. Putnam as the party's last-minute candidates for governor and representative.[59] This procedure gave the Democrats an additional aura of democratic respectability.

In the ensuing campaign Levy and Call were the major opponents, though running for different offices. The Whigs concentrated their attack against Levy on the assumption that his victory would probably mean a Democratic sweep, including that of the new state legislature.[60] "Opposition to Democracy," they cried, "is obedience to God."[61] Call and Putnam were characterized as "the Laboring Man's candidates—the Poor Man's friends—the People's Choice."[62] To spread the Whig gospel Colonel Isaiah D. Hart of Duval County created the *Florida Whig and Peoples Advocate*. But beyond personal invective and ridicule, particularly where Levy was concerned, the Whig leaders and editors found few weapons effective against what they denounced as the loco-foco attack.

The Democratic organization, on the other hand, conducted a far more effective campaign. Local leaders were spurred on to greater efforts. Levy recognized the Whig strategy. "To reduce me was the only means of reducing the Legislative ticket," he wrote Westcott. He effectively counteracted the attack and then went on to bolster Moseley's position. Levy explained to Westcott that "It was necessary to make a bold stroke to save him [Moseley], in consequence of his not coming to the East where he was an utter stranger. . . . I drew the party lines strictly. . . . By making a direct party issue, I planted my friends in solid column. . . . By this means I secured for the whole ticket my own vote—and by attacking Call I secured for Moseley all the additional vote which prejudice agst C[all] would give him."[63] Though not a particularly modest analysis, it was accurate. The Democrats insisted at the outset that nothing should be concealed from the people. Nothing past or present pertaining to the Whigs was. The Democrats attacked "dishonest bank directors" and "swindling speculators"; they faithfully and unnecessarily raised

59. Doherty, *The Whigs of Florida*, p. 15.
60. W. J. Watt [?] to J. M. Berrien, April 28, 1845, B. A. Putnam to J. M. Berrien, August 5, 1845 (Berrien Papers, University of North Carolina); D. Levy to J. D. Westcott, Jr., May 29, 1845 (copy, Yulee Papers).
61. Pensacola *Gazette*, June 7, 1845.
62. Apalachicola *Commercial Advertiser*, May 17, 1845.
63. D. Levy to J. D. Westcott, Jr., May 29, 1845 (copy, Yulee Papers).

the spectre of the faith bonds; they ridiculed Call's references to his military background and connections with Andrew Jackson; they took a firm stand in favor of taxing "men according to the quantity of land they possess, according to the number of hands they work, according to the style and grandeur of their equipages."[64] President Polk's assurance that no Florida offices would be filled until after the election also helped to bring the wavering voter with any job aspirations into the Democratic ranks.[65]

The probable results of the election became increasingly apparent, so much so that East Florida's leading Whig newspaper, the St. Augustine *News*, changed to Democratic hands. The Tallahassee *Star of Florida* also gave up hope, abandoning the Whig course in favor of neutrality and describing the entire affair as "barbecue electioneering" with the "candidates eating their way into the favor of the dear people."[66] In May, Moseley defeated Call for the governorship by over five hundred votes, while Levy rolled up a majority more than twice as large over Putnam. The Democrats captured both houses of the first General Assembly, winning thirty of the House's forty-one seats and eleven of the Senate's seventeen.[67]

Having been a salient factor in his party's victory, Levy now aspired to membership in the United States Senate. This was hardly unexpected. The Whigs had earlier called this political play on the part of the Democrats, and Levy himself had been a partner in its making.[68] Indeed, some East Florida Democratic county meetings had selected their candidates for the General Assembly with the understanding that Levy would have their support for the Senate.[69] As soon as his election to the House of Representatives was confirmed, therefore, most of the Democratic press began to boom him for the upper chamber. Even the neutral *Star of Florida* approved, though rejecting the prospect of Westcott as the second senator.[70] But there were dissenting voices in the Democratic party; other leaders aspired to high office too. Levy decided it would be

64. St. Augustine *Florida Herald*, May 20, 1845; St. Augustine *News*, May 3, 10, 1845; D. Levy to J. D. Westcott, Jr., April 13, 1845 (copy, Yulee Papers).

65. D. Levy to J. D. Westcott, Jr., March 21, April 13, 1845 (copies, Yulee Papers); D. Levy to J. K. Polk, April 5, 1845 (Polk Papers, Library of Congress).     66. May 16, 1845.

67. See tables 1, 2, and 3.

68. Pensacola *Gazette*, May 17, 1845; Tallahassee *Florida Sentinel*, May 3, 1845; D. Levy to J. D. Westcott, Jr., April 13, May 29, 1845 (copies, Yulee Papers).     69. St. Augustine *News*, April 19, 1845.

70. June 20, 1845.

well to have another postponement of federal appointments, and Polk complied.[71]

Levy then journeyed to Tallahassee in time for the meeting of the General Assembly which convened on June 23. He immediately found himself in the middle of a full-blown party conflict and then inadvertently thrust himself into the midst of another. John Branch meant to be one of Florida's new senators. He had had a long and varied career, his first major office coming as governor of North Carolina in 1817. He later served as that state's senator from 1823 to 1829 and as Jackson's Secretary of the Navy from 1829 to 1831. In Florida he had been an early opponent of the banks, as well as the last territorial governor.[72] Levy had assumed Branch would also be the first Democratic candidate for state governor, but he did not get the nomination. Unfortunately, all the twists and turns of that state convention are not known, and it is impossible to say with any certainty whether he passed up the governorship in favor of striking for senator or whether Westcott's Middle Florida forces had simply bushwhacked him in favor of Moseley. In either case, Branch was now ready for the Senate. When Levy reached Tallahassee, he found himself rather "indelicately . . . beset by Gov. Branch and his friends" who were eager to upset Mr. Westcott's aspirations.[73] Levy's neutrality alienated Branch and annoyed Westcott. Then, to compound the confusion, West Florida's Walker Anderson clashed with Westcott. This time Levy stepped in and attempted to restore more friendly relations between the two, only to discover that Anderson also had his eye on the Senate, and efforts to heal the breach proved fruitless.[74]

By the end of June, 1845, therefore, the Democrats had four eager candidates for the Senate of the United States, with only the usual two seats available. At the party caucus of June 30 the supporters of Branch and Anderson teamed up against Levy and Westcott. The final vote was 20 to 17 against Branch and Anderson. On July 1 Levy and Westcott went on to defeat the Whig candidates, Joseph M. Hernandez and Jackson Morton, by a straight party vote of 41 to 16.[75] The disappointed Democratic candidates undoubtedly re-

71. D. Levy to J. K. Polk, June 9, 1845 (Polk Papers, Library of Congress).
72. Carter, *Florida Territory*, pp. 584-85.
73. D. Levy to J. D. Westcott, Jr., October 20, 1845 (copy, Yulee Papers).
74. *Ibid.*
75. Tallahassee *Star of Florida*, July 1, 1845; St. Augustine *News*, July 12, 1845.

sented Levy. After all, had he remained in the House, one of them would have been senator. On July 11 Moseley probably sought to justify Levy's shift when he addressed a special letter to the legislature. He brought their attention to Article I, Section 4, of the Constitution of the United States which provided that the state legislature prescribed "the Times, Places and Manner of holding Elections for Senators and Representatives." Levy's election to the House had taken place prior to the first legislative session under rules established in 1838 by the St. Joseph Convention and would ultimately have been declared invalid.[76]

The political organization of the new state was finally completed and Levy could write Polk that Florida had entered the Union with a "thoroughly Democratic organization." Now, too, the delayed distribution of spoils could proceed, with the President's cooperation.[77] That fall William H. Brockenbrough filled Levy's vacated House seat by defeating Edward C. Cabell, a rising Whig star from West Florida, despite the complication of a disputed election.[78]

The Jacksonian Democrats had reached the apex of their power in Florida. It was perhaps symbolic that during the evening of June 23, 1845, on the first day of the first state legislative session, news reached the assembled Democratic leaders in Tallahassee of the death of Andrew Jackson.[79]

76. St. Augustine *News*, July 26, 1845.
77. D. Levy to J. K. Polk, June 9, July 16, August n.d., 1845 (Polk Papers, Library of Congress).
78. D. Levy to J. K. Polk, September 25, 1845 (Polk Papers); Tallahassee *Star of Florida*, October 17, 31, 1845.
79. Tallahassee *Star of Florida*, June 27, 1845.

# 7. TRANSITION

After 1845 the Democratic party in Florida underwent a series of significant changes. New issues arose, the party's focus shifted, and its basic philosophy was transformed. During the early years of its ascendancy between 1839 and 1842 most of the party's leaders were younger, less calculating politicians, its outlook was far less Southern, and both its framework and sympathies were more honestly democratic. By the 1850's much of this was reversed. In the long run this shift had its origins in the conflict which stemmed from the aftereffects of "Jeffersonian Republicanism" and the emergence of "Jacksonian Democracy." The Jackson movement had been composed of disparate elements and forces, among them the divergent trends reflected in the split between Andrew Jackson and John C. Calhoun. It was this breach, symbolized by the conflict over nullification, that had a strange and delayed impact on Florida politics.

In the 1830's Florida, and particularly East Florida, was as much frontier as Southern in its general complexion. It was also still a territory. As a consequence, states' rights, nullification, and secession were virtually nonexistent issues. The emerging elite of the new area, though composed of Jackson men, were not Jacksonian Democrats, and they gradually broke away from Jackson and Van Buren on a variety of fronts. But on the question of nullification and the Union their ranks were virtually unbroken in support of Old Hickory. When James Gadsden supported Calhoun in the South Carolina controversy, he was pushed aside in the 1833 race for delegate and Richard K. Call himself entered the lists. But those who opposed Call and the early Jackson men—those who were soon to emerge as the Democratic party—did not in that opposition accept the Calhoun position on nullification. Instead, it was on the antibank drive, temporarily obscuring the statehood question, that the Democratic offensive was mounted. Significant, too, was the fact that the antibank stand of the Democrats was not based on the narrow constitutional grounds of states' rights. Rather their enthusiastic attack against chartered monopolies, special privilege, aristocracy, and a political elite finally brought the Jacksonian Democratic movement to Florida. In a few years the bank issue subsided and the party experienced political reverses. Then the statehood issue came to be of paramount importance, contributing to its revival in 1844 as well as to triumph and statehood in 1845.

Statehood, however, had unforeseen consequences, for nothing affected the mutation of the Democratic party in Washington and in Florida more than the increasing pressure of the intersectional controversy during the late 1840's. The "transition" was also accelerated by the second and final Whig revival after 1846, which produced considerable anxiety among the leaders of the Democratic party.[1] As a result, the political challenge at home was met by taking a far more extreme position during the crisis of 1850 than the Democrats might otherwise have assumed. In so doing, they were able to tar the Florida Whigs for having feathered their nest with northern abolitionism. Thus, the hardening of sectional lines provided the Democrats in Florida with still a new—and their most dangerous—weapon.

Throughout the first secession crisis Whig leaders pursued a course of moderation and appealed in vain to the "Jacksonian Democrats," taunting them with deserting Jackson's stand of the early thirties against Calhoun, nullification, and secession threats.[2] But the Democratic party ardently supported the Nashville Convention and opposed the Compromise measures of Congress before and after their adoption.[3] The entire crisis seemed to offer too much political capital which could be used against the resurgent Whigs for the Democrats to alter their new direction. But widespread popular meetings in support of the Compromise even in East Florida, Edward C. Cabell's re-election to a third congressional term in 1850, and David Levy's defeat for re-election to the Senate in 1851 forced the Democrats to pause temporarily and reassess their position on the issue.[4]

Events, however, were moving in their favor. Despite the popularity of the Compromise, the Whig position in Florida was being undermined by the decline of its national organization. Democrats took advantage of their opponents' dilemma in the elections of 1852 by completely reversing their stand on the Compromise, while continuing their pro-Southern sentiments. As a result, they

1. Doherty, *The Whigs of Florida*, p. 2.
2. Doherty, "Florida and the Crisis of 1850," *Journal of Southern History*, XIX (February, 1953), 32.
3. Thompson, "David L. Yulee," pp. 42-52.
4. Only in part can Levy's defeat be attributed to his stand on the Compromise.—Thompson, "The Railroad Background of the Florida Senatorial Election of 1851," *Florida Historical Quarterly*, XXXI (January, 1953), 192-93.

won over some Union sympathizers and still held on to their states' rights supporters.[5]

Thus, the Florida Democrats who had earlier adhered to the general economic and social philosophy of Jacksonianism now resolved their position on the Jackson-Calhoun conflict by adopting the political position of the latter. But Call and many of those who had become Whigs maintained their Unionist positions; indeed, in the 1850's they shifted from one new political group to another in an almost frantic effort to curb the increasingly radical Southern outlook of the Democratic party.[6]

A number of factors during the 1850's strengthened the control of the "radical" wing in the Democratic party. Aside from those forces which were also operative in other Southern states, the new tide of immigration into Florida was of considerable importance. These migrants came almost exclusively from the lower South. They brought with them those conscious and already well-formed ideas which increased the "Southernization" of the Florida Democracy. In the meantime, too, as a larger number of Middle and West Florida planters came to rest in the Democratic party, some of the small agrarians—resenting this wealthier intrusion—reluctantly found a haven in the anti-Democratic movements of 1856 and 1858. Others withdrew from politics completely, some even leaving the state and the south. The varied reactions of these disaffected Jacksonians undoubtedly eased the task of the secessionists in achieving a dominant voice in the state Democratic party.[7]

Finally, it might be suggested here that the emotional crusade of the Jacksonian Democrats during the early 1840's had its residuum in the equally emotional states'-rights crusade of the 1850's. Yet there was a basic difference. The earlier concern with the rights of individuals had increasingly been subordinated to an emphasis on the rights of the state. Moreover, the Jackson era had produced men who, in their efforts to broaden the base of political participation and to achieve a freer form of enterprise, were altering legal precedent along with the traditions of established property and contractual relations—men who denounced bitterly those who would use the state to promote individual economic pursuits. Their goals too would be impeded by the states'-rights movement that so many

5. John Meador, "Florida and the Compromise of 1850," *Florida Historical Quarterly*, XXXIX (July, 1960), 29.

6. Thompson, "Political Nativism in Florida," pp. 58-65.

7. Thompson, "David L. Yulee," p. 132.

of them blindly advocated. But this latter cause would receive an earlier revival than that of the other facet of Jacksonianism which was abandoned, for in the decades which immediately preceded and followed the Civil War some of those young entrepreneurs were to develop into relatively powerful industrial capitalists. It was no paradox, therefore, that most of them would join with their earlier Whig opponents not only during the hectic era after the War, but also in the Compromise of 1877 which ended Reconstruction.

TABLE 1.—TERRITORIAL (1840-44) AND STATE (1845) SENATE ELECTIONS

| | 1840 | | 1842 | | 1844 | | 1845 | |
|---|---|---|---|---|---|---|---|---|
| | Dem. | "Whig" | Dem. | Whig | Dem. | Whig | Dem. | Whig |
| East Florida | 4 | 0 | 3 | 1 | 3 | 3 | 5 | 1 |
| Middle Florida | 0 | 4 | 1 | 4 | 5 | 0 | 4 | 2 |
| West Florida | 0 | 3 | 1 | 3 | 1 | 3 | 2 | 3 |
| Total | 4 | 7 | 5 | 8 | 9 | 6 | 11 | 6 |

*Sources:*

1840—Tallahassee *Floridian,* October 17, 31, 1840; St. Augustine *Florida Herald,* October 17, November 20, 1840; Quincy *Sentinel,* October 23, 1840.

1842—Pensacola *Gazette,* October 15, 22, 1842; St. Augustine *News,* October 29, November 5, 1842; Tallahassee *Florida Sentinel,* October 14, 28, November 11, 1842.

1844—St. Augustine *News,* November 16, 30, December 7, 1844; St. Augustine *Florida Herald,* November 19, 1844; Pensacola *Gazette,* November 9, 1844; Apalachicola *Commercial Advertiser,* November 5, December 7, 1844.

1845—Tallahassee *Star of Florida,* June 20, 1845; St. Augustine *News,* June 7, 1845.

TABLE 2.—TERRITORIAL (1839-44) AND STATE (1845) HOUSE ELECTIONS

| | 1839 | | 1840 | | 1841 | | 1842 | | 1843 | | 1844 | | 1845 | |
|---|---|---|---|---|---|---|---|---|---|---|---|---|---|---|
| | Dem. | "Whig" | Dem. | "Whig" | Dem. | Whig | Dem. | Whig | Dem. | Whig | Dem. | Whig | Dem. | Whig |
| St. Johns | 0 | 2 | 2 | 0 | 2 | 0 | 2 | 0 | 2 | 0 | 2 | 0 | 3 | 0 |
| Columbia | 0 | 1 | 1 | 0 | 1 | 0 | 0 | 1 | 1 | 0 | 1 | 0 | 2 | 0 |
| Alachua | 1 | 0 | 1 | 0 | 1 | 0 | 0 | 1 | 1 | 0 | 1 | 1c | 2 | 0 |
| Duval | 1 | 1 | 2 | 0 | 0 | 1c | 0 | 1c | 0 | 2 | 1 | 1c | 2 | 1 |
| Nassau | 1 | 0 | 1 | 0 | 0 | 1c | 0 | 1c | 0 | 1 | 0 | 1 | 0 | 0 |
| Mosquito (Orange) | 1 | 0 | 1 | 0 | 1 | 0 | 0 | 1c | 0 | 1 | 1b | 0 | 1 | 0 |
| Hillsborough | 1 | 0 | 1 | 0 | 1 | 0 | 1b | 0 | 1 | 0 | 0 | 1 | 1 | 0 |
| Monroe | 1 | 0 | 1 | 0 | 1 | 0 | 0 | 1 | 0 | 1 | 1 | 0 | 1 | 0 |
| Dade | | 1a | 1 | 0 | 1 | 0 | 1 | 0 | 1 | 0 | 0 | 1 | 1 | 0 |
| Benton | … | … | … | … | … | … | … | … | … | … | 1 | 0 | g | 0 |
| Marion | … | … | … | … | … | … | … | … | … | … | 1 | 1 | h | 0 |
| St. Lucie | … | … | … | … | … | … | … | … | … | … | 0 | 0 | … | … |
| East Florida total | 6 | 4 | 11 | 0 | 9 | 2 | 5 | 6 | 6 | 5 | 9f | 4f | 13 | 1 |
| Leon | 4 | 0 | 1 | 3 | 4 | 0 | 5 | 0 | 0 | 5 | 0 | 3 | 12 | 3 |
| Jefferson | 2 | 0 | 2 | 0 | 2 | 0 | 2 | 1 | 2 | 0 | 2 | 1 | 3 | 3 |
| Madison | 0 | 1 | 1 | 0 | 0 | 0 | 1 | 0 | 1 | 0 | 1 | 0 | 1 | 0 |
| Hamilton | 1 | 0 | 0 | 1 | 1 | 1 | 1 | 1 | 0 | 1 | 0 | 1 | 1 | 1 |
| Gadsden | 1 | 1 | 0 | 2 | 0 | 2 | 0 | 2 | 1e | 2 | 2 | 0 | 2 | 2 |
| Wakulla | … | … | … | … | … | … | … | … | 1 | 0 | 1 | 0 | i | 0 |
| Middle Florida total | 8 | 2 | 4 | 6 | 7 | 3 | 4 | 6 | 5 | 4 | 6 | 4 | 12 | 3 |
| Escambia | 2 | 0 | 2 | 0 | 2b | 0 | 0 | 1 | 0 | 1 | 0 | 1 | 0 | 3 |
| Jackson | 2 | 0 | 0 | 2 | 0 | 2 | 1 | 1 | 1 | 2 | 2 | 2 | 0 | 3 |
| Walton | 0 | 1 | 0 | 1 | 1 | 0 | 1 | 1 | 0 | 1 | 0 | 1 | 1 | 0 |
| Washington | 1 | 0 | 1 | 0 | 1 | 0 | 1 | 0 | 1 | 0 | 1 | 0 | 1 | 0 |
| Calhoun | 1 | 1 | 1d | 0 | 1 | 0 | 1 | 0 | 1 | 0 | 1 | 0 | 2 | 0 |
| Franklin | 0 | 1 | 0 | 1 | 0 | 1 | 0 | 1 | 0 | 1 | 0 | 1 | 2 | 0 |
| Santa Rosa | … | … | … | … | … | … | … | … | … | … | 0 | 1 | j | 0 |
| West Florida total | 6 | 2 | 4 | 2 | 5 | 3 | 4 | 4 | 3 | 5 | 3 | 5 | 5 | 7 |
| **Total** | 20 | 8 | 19 | 10 | 21 | 8 | 13 | 16 | 14 | 14 | 18 | 13 | 30 | 11 |

*Sources:* 1839—St. Joseph *Times,* October 15, 1839; St. Augustine *Florida Herald,* November 15, 1839. 1840—Tallahassee *Floridian,* October 17, 31, 1840; St. Augustine *Florida Herald,* October 17, November 20, 1840; Quincy *Sentinel,* October 23, 1840. 1841—Tallahassee *Florida Sentinel,* October 15, 1841; St. Augustine *Florida Herald,* October 15, November 5, 12, 1841; Pensacola *Gazette,* September 25, October 16, 23, 1841; St. Augustine *News,* October 17, 1841; Tallahassee *Floridian,* October 16, 1841. 1842—Pensacola *Gazette,* October 15, 1842; St. Augustine *News,* October 15, 22, 29, November 5, December 10, 1842; Tallahassee *Florida Sentinel,* October 14, 21, 28, November 11, 25, 1842. 1843—Tallahassee *Florida Sentinel,* October and November, 1843; January 2, 1844; St. Augustine *News,* November 11, 25, December 2, 9, 16, 1843, January 13, 1844; Tallahassee *Floridian,* November 18, 1843. 1844—St. Augustine *Florida Herald,* December 17, 1844; St. Augustine *News,* November 16, 23, 30, December 7, 1844; Tallahassee *Star of Florida,* January 10, 1845; Apalachicola *Commercial Advertiser,* December 7, 1844. 1845—Tallahassee *Star of Florida,* May 30, June 20, 1845.

a—no party information available; b—very likely a Democrat; c—very likely a Whig; d—pro-bank Democrat; e—independent candidate; f—additional representation for east Florida from newly created counties was challenged; g—included with Alachua County; h—included with Orange County; i—included with Leon County; j—included with Escambia County.

**TABLE 3.—TERRITORY- AND STATE-WIDE ELECTIONS, 1839-1845**

| | 1839 | | | | 1841 | | | 1843 | | 1845 | | | |
|---|---|---|---|---|---|---|---|---|---|---|---|---|---|
| | Delegate | | Constitution | | Delegate | | | Delegate | | Governer | | U. S. Represent. | |
| | Baltzell | Downing | Yes | Nó | Levy | Ward | Downing | Levy | Ward | Moseley | Call | Levy | Putnam |
| St. Johns | 8 | 328 | 91 | 246 | 216 | 16 | 136 | 213 | 93 | 173 | 117 | 171 | 125 |
| Columbia | 11 | 202 | 41 | 161 | 302/122 | 24/29 | 189/79 | 243 | 45 | 349 | 128 | 355 | 132 |
| Alachua | 10 | 129 | 100 | 6 | 129/259 | 7/20 | 40/44 | 253 | 58 | 193 | 91 | 193 | 94 |
| Duval | 9 | 332 | 42 | 296 | 162/192 | 33/44 | 158/211 | 217 | 126 | 235 | 156 | 232 | 162 |
| Nassau | 2 | 94 | ? | 51 | 49 | 0 | 14 | 89 | 20 | 129 | 23 | 127 | 27 |
| Mosquito | ? | ? | ? | ? | 4 | 0 | 0 | 42 | 25 | 28 | 10 | 29 | 10 |
| Hillsborough | 59 | 46 | 56 | 49 | 16 | 50 | 1 | 51 | 15 | 24 | 14 | 28 | 10 |
| Monroe | 5 | 108 | 97 | 11 | 6 | 12 | 116 | 151 | 14 | 101/157 | 44/73 | 101/156 | 45/72 |
| Dade | 0 | 72 | 64 | 8 | 10 | 0 | 0 | 16 | 4 | 60 | 74 | 60 | 5 |
| Marion | — | — | — | — | — | — | — | — | — | 94 | 4 | 93 | 75 |
| Benton | — | — | — | — | — | — | — | — | — | 78 | 1 | 78 | 8 |
| St. Lucie | — | — | — | — | — | — | — | — | — | 16 | — | 16 | 1 |
| East Florida total | 104 | 1311 | 491 | 828 | 844 | 160 | 601 | 1361 | 409 | 1536 | 696 | 1538 | 721 |
| Leon | 461 | 225 | 482 | 142 | 293/307 | 302 | 56 | 226 | 284 | 269 | 321 | 301 | 286 |
| Jefferson | 340 | 64 | 322 | 51 | 221 | 144 | 3 | 263 | 84 | 256 | 149 | 332 | 77 |
| Madison | 109 | 40 | 51 | 16 | 115 | 99 | 0 | 107 | 79 | 174 | 124 | 215 | 79 |
| Hamilton | 11 | 60 | 19 | 51 | 64 | 10 | 33 | 104 | 49 | 89 | 11 | 90 | 11 |
| Wakulla | — | — | — | — | 88 | 56 | 48 | 121 | 38 | 88 | 78 | 119 | 51 |
| Gadsden | 322 | 115 | 204 | 95 | 84 | 209/215 | 34/81 | 182 | 277 | 230 | 279 | 264 | 251 |
| Middle Florida total | 1243 | 504 | 1078 | 355 | 815 | 816 | 237 | 1003 | 811 | 1106 | 962 | 1321 | 755 |
| Escambia | 62 | 199 | 30 | 193 | 45 | 148 | 32 | 130 | 108 | 96 | 171 | 105 | 162 |
| Jackson | 388 | 62 | 247 | 114 | 123 | 197/213 | 12 | 91 | 214 | 130 | 332 | 162 | 300 |
| Walton | 33 | 28 | 38 | 27 | ? | ? | ? | 47 | 96 | 64 | 202 | 101 | 167 |
| Washington | 47 | 24 | 16 | 53 | 41 | 9 | 7 | 55 | 5 | 86 | 11 | 92 | 5 |
| Calhoun | 15 | 326 | 73 | 275 | 39 | 71 | 11 | 49 | 15 | 46 | 6 | 48 | 1 |
| Franklin | 88 | 141 | 92 | 116 | 39 | 75/91 | 63/67 | 104 | 148 | 113 | 106 | 119 | 98 |
| Santa Rosa | — | — | — | — | — | — | — | 20 | 79 | 29 | 137 | 35 | 131 |
| West Florida total | 633 | 780 | 496 | 778 | 300 | 538 | 129 | 496 | 665 | 566 | 962 | 659 | 864 |
| Total | 1980 | 2595 | 2065 | 1961 | 1959 | 1514 | 967 | 2807 | 1737 | 3115 | 2602 | 3422 | 2325 |

Sources: 1839—St. Augustine Florida Herald, August 29, 1839; St. Augustine Florida News, October 18, 1839; Quincy Sentinel, February 10, 1841; St. Joseph Times, June 1, 1839. 1841—Tallahassee Floridian, May 29, 1841; St. Augustine Florida Herald, June 11, 1841; St. Augustine Florida News, June 18, 1841. 1843—St. Augustine Florida Herald, June 5, 1843. 1845—Tallahassee Star of Florida, June 20, 1845.

County votes and district totals have been compiled from a variety of sources. Moreover, in some elections, particularly 1841, dual returns are available. As a consequence, regional and total tabulations are not always consistent with the sum of county returns.

TABLE 4.—FLORIDA JACKSONIAN LEADERSHIP
## AGE CLASSIFICATION

| Age Groups | East Florida | Middle Florida | West Florida | Total | Per Cent |
|---|---|---|---|---|---|
| 20's | 13 | 17 | 2 | 32 | 21 |
| 30's | 24 | 35 | 10 | 69 | 46 |
| 40's | 13 | 23 | 4 | 40 | 27 |
| 50's | 5 | 2 | 1 | 8 | 5 |
| 60's | 1 | 0 | 0 | 1 | 1 |

*Source*: Microfilm copies of the original schedules of the Sixth Census of the United States, 1840, in the P. K. Yonge Library of Florida History, University of Florida.

TABLE 5.—FLORIDA JACKSONIAN LEADERSHIP
SLAVE OWNERSHIP

| | No Slaves | 1-5 Slaves | Over 5 Slaves | Per Cent No Slaves | Per Cent Slaves |
|---|---|---|---|---|---|
| East Florida | 14 | 16 | 23 | 26 | 74 |
| Middle Florida | 9 | 15 | 42 | 14 | 86 |
| West Florida* | 3 | 2 | 6 | 27 | 73 |
| Total | 26 | 33 | 71 | 20 | 80 |

*Source*: Microfilm copies of the original schedules of the Sixth Census of the United States, 1840.

*Three counties of West Florida did not list individual slaveholding figures.

TABLE 6.—FLORIDA JACKSONIAN LEADERSHIP
OCCUPATION BREAKDOWNS

| | East Florida | Middle Florida | West Florida* | Total | Per Cent |
|---|---|---|---|---|---|
| Large planter | 1 | 7 | 0 | 8 | 7 |
| Small planter | 7 | 29 | 0 | 36 | 30 |
| Manufacturing and trade (incl. artisans) | 5 | 13 | 3 | 21 | 18 |
| Professional | 9 | 14 | 5 | 28 | 23 |
| Commerce (inland & ocean) | 1 | 8 | 1 | 10 | 8 |
| Yeoman farmer | 9 | 8 | 0 | 17 | 14 |

*Source*: Microfilm copies of the original schedules of the Sixth Census of the United States, 1840, in the P. K. Yonge Library, University of Florida.

*Three counties of West Florida had no occupational breakdown.

UNIVERSITY OF FLORIDA MONOGRAPHS

*Social Sciences*

No. 1 (Winter 1959): *The Whigs of Florida, 1845-1854*
By Herbert J. Doherty, Jr.

No. 2 (Spring 1959): *Austrian Catholics and the Social Question, 1918-1933*
By Alfred Diamant

No. 3 (Summer 1959): *The Siege of St. Augustine in 1702*
By Charles W. Arnade

No. 4 (Fall 1959): *New Light on Early and Medieval Japanese Historiography*
Two Translations and an Introduction
By John A. Harrison

No. 5 (Winter 1960): *The Swiss Press and Foreign Affairs in World War II*
By Frederick H. Hartmann

No. 6 (Spring 1960): *The American Militia Decade of Decision, 1789-1800*
By John K. Mahon

No. 7 (Summer 1960): *The Foundation of Jacques Maritain's Political Philosophy*
By Hwa Yol Jung

No. 8 (Fall 1960): *Latin American Population Studies*
By T. Lynn Smith

No. 9 (Winter 1961): *Jacksonian Democracy on the Florida Frontier*
By Arthur W. Thompson